THE AGE OF SCIENCE-TECH UNIVERSITIES

Analysing past and ongoing trends that have shaped the landscape of universities worldwide, this book explores the possible paths for the future of universities along three main dimensions characterizing key strategic choices: knowledge creation and dissemination, relationships within society and governance mechanisms.

By sharing reflections and offering directions on the changing role of technical universities, especially in Europe, this book considers the change and disruption that are causing universities to reconsider their role.

This book:

- provides an up-to-date picture of the role of technical universities in the European context
- critically discusses the strengths and weaknesses of technical universities
- identifies emerging challenges that will shape their evolution going forward
- provides insight into how current models can be adapted and adopted for future use

Impinging on extensive transdisciplinary research, this book highlights the need of the technical university within society and its role not only to improve skills, but education in the most articulated sense, to train future citizens and professionals. The book is a must-read for all those interested in the future of technical universities.

Paola Francesca Antonietti, Paola Bertola, Antonio Capone, Bianca Maria Colosimo, Davide Moscatelli, Carolina Pacchi and Stefano Ronchi are Professors at Politecnico di Milano with expertise ranging from urban planning to mechanics, from design to chemistry. Together they form PoliMI 2040, a team built to support the strategic decision-making process by developing possible future scenarios.

THE AGE OF SCIENCE-TECH UNIVERSITIES

Responsibilities, Challenges and Strategies

Paola Francesca Antonietti, Paola Bertola, Antonio Capone, Bianca Maria Colosimo, Davide Moscatelli, Carolina Pacchi and Stefano Ronchi

LONDON AND NEW YORK

Cover image: © Getty Images

First published 2022
by Routledge
2 Park Square, Milton Park, Abingdon, Oxon, OX14 4RN

and by Routledge
605 Third Avenue, New York, NY 10158

Routledge is an imprint of the Taylor & Francis Group, an informa business

© 2022 Paola Francesca Antonietti, Paola Bertola, Antonio Capone, Bianca Maria Colosimo, Davide Moscatelli, Carolina Pacchi and Stefano Ronchi

The right of Paola Francesca Antonietti, Paola Bertola, Antonio Capone, Bianca Maria Colosimo, Davide

Moscatelli, Carolina Pacchi and Stefano Ronchi to be identified as author[/s] of this work has been asserted in accordance with sections 77 and 78 of the Copyright, Designs and Patents Act 1988.

All rights reserved. No part of this book may be reprinted or reproduced or utilised in any form or by any electronic, mechanical, or other means, now known or hereafter invented, including photocopying and recording, or in any information storage or retrieval system, without permission in writing from the publishers.

Trademark notice: Product or corporate names may be trademarks or registered trademarks, and are used only for identification and explanation without intent to infringe.

British Library Cataloguing-in-Publication Data

A catalogue record for this book is available from the British Library

Library of Congress Cataloging-in-Publication Data
A catalog record for this title has been requested

ISBN: 978-1-032-13834-3 (hbk)
ISBN: 978-1-032-13835-0 (pbk)
ISBN: 978-1-003-23100-4 (ebk)

DOI: 10.4324/9781003231004

Typeset in Bembo
by Apex CoVantage, LLC

CONTENTS

Preface   *vii*

Acknowledgements   *ix*

Introduction   1

1   Universities and their challenges in a changing world   9

1.1 Dynamics of development and evolution in universities 10

1.2 Work, skills and education in the knowledge society 16

1.3 National economies, local hubs and models of research and innovation 21

1.4 Current trends and today's challenges for universities 25

2   Education, research, entrepreneurship, society:
Comparing models   33

2.1 Education poised between disciplinarity and new pedagogical approaches 36

2.2 Scientific research poised between impact and exploring new frontiers 44

2.3 University entrepreneurship within emerging innovation paradigms 56

2.4 Universities' role and their projection in society 69

vi Contents

3 Governance in universities 78

3.1 Interaction between university and government 78
3.2 University governance models 80

4 Strategic choices for universities of science and technology 89

4.1 Knowledge – its forms, objectives and how it develops 90
*4.2 Relationships – actors interacting in the university
system 103*
4.3 System – choosing the organization model 121

5 Conclusions 135

5.1 Coherence within strategic decisions 135
5.2 Influence of the context of reference 136
5.3 Potential discontinuity 140
5.4 Governing the dynamics of change 143

Index *145*

PREFACE

Since I have started my mandate at the helm of Politecnico di Milano, I immediately realized the needs and demands of complex organizations. Universities make no difference, especially those oriented towards research and innovation. Particularly those aiming at contributing to a sustainable socio-economic impact shaping the future of next generations.

Indeed, education is a multifaceted industry that, just like all the others, needs a compass to support strategic directions. For this reason, together with a group of very committed colleagues, we decided to give birth to a cross-disciplinary team involving a number of departments of our university in order to stimulate an internal and external debate about future challenges and possible crossroads.

This was the beginning of the PoliMI 2040 project in 2017, whose outcomes are reported in this book. Of course, there have been key contextual and long-term factors influencing the project. The first one, no question, is the speed of technology, especially information technology, its acceleration and consequent driving force. Evolution is becoming exponential and disruptive, making it mandatory to anticipate the change rather than being guided by it.

What is more, we are becoming more and more aware that global challenges – such as the ones dealing with the environment or energy consumption, cyber threats or artificial intelligence, just to mention a few of them – require a multidisciplinary approach. For instance, we cannot face the future of mobility if we do not consider engineering when it comes to new vehicles, but also sociology when developing targeted services, as well as law and philosophy when asked to decide on ethical questions, such as the ones belonging to algorithms functioning in autonomous driving.

Last but not least, we are more and more aware that, in a global context, competition relies on cooperation. Europe, which should be the third actor in the worldwide scene, recently experienced the failure of policies implemented by centrifugal

viii Preface

forces, gradually appearing more isolated and less influential. However, in the last year and a half, Europe has implemented extensive supportive measures and fostered common policies and research networks as a reaction to Covid-19 pandemic, a lesson learned at a very high cost.

As a matter of fact, while accomplishing PoliMI 2040 project, we found ourselves working alongside the rampant coronavirus pandemic. Some of the ongoing processes of change took off at a greater pace. The emergency also stimulated a renewed interest in science and in innovation, seen as the only possible way to cope with complicated problems suddenly affecting the entire planet. Therefore, many assumptions and trends analysed during the course of our study have been rapidly corroborated and eventually proved to be right.

Academia too went through a process of self-analysis, a very quick one. The unexpected Covid-19 outbreak forced us to react rapidly and efficiently to the crisis by turning all our courses online. Despite and also because of a very unstable scenario, we did what we could to keep our labs open to help institutions and industries on the front line against the virus. We enforced our alliances with foreign universities and drew common plans despite mobility being put to a halt.

Now time has come to look ahead and plan for the future. When I say this, I am not referring to immediate solutions, rather our ability to seize a big opportunity for the world to change the way we teach, learn, work and interact. We are now asking ourselves what kind of knowledge will be developed, how are relationships going to change, and how will the whole system adapt to a post-pandemic reality.

As such, every university will revise their programmes, finding new ways to engage students and bringing about additional business models, confirming the fact that the new millennium has opened the way to new prospects, especially for science-tech universities. Academia must urgently shoulder greater responsibility for the broadly unexplored impacts that scientific and technical innovation may have in its current form and commit themselves more firmly to action.

The outcomes described in this book have already inspired a series of choices within Politecnico di Milano itself, which are included in the current university's strategic plan. Nevertheless, if there is one lesson we have learned from this pandemic, it is that no one can make it alone. Hence, I believe that this book might be a useful guide for other institutions, as well as policymakers and stakeholders engaged in development processes that underline the pivotal role of higher education and knowledge, to lead a well-balanced, responsible and long-lasting change.

Ferruccio Resta
Rector, Politecnico di Milano

ACKNOWLEDGEMENTS

This book is the result of an intensive four-year project involving a very high number of people; listing everyone would be almost impossible.

First of all, we would like to thank the Rector of Politecnico di Milano, and the Institution overall for trusting us and giving us the opportunity to work together on such a challenging project. Thanks to Vice-Rectors, Deans, Directors and all colleagues who were actively involved in interviews and discussions. These interactions gave us the great opportunity to understand and appreciate our university even more.

We would also like to thank colleagues from other universities around the globe. Discussing and debating with inspiring characters in leadership roles at other universities has been a source of keen insights for this book.

Finally, we would like to thank members of our Advisory Board, alumni from our university with high seniority, experience and international visibility, for their valuable and visionary comments and inputs to our work.

In a nutshell, thanks to Politecnico di Milano and its international network.

INTRODUCTION

Early universities first saw the light of day in Mediaeval Europe, their roots firmly implanted in Roman Catholic congregations with flourishing monastic schools of philosophy, theology and the humanities more widely. With the onset of the First Industrial Revolution and under the inspiration of illuminism, universities were remodelled to place greater emphasis on scientific subjects and studies, helping the progress of ongoing technological development. During the Second Industrial Revolution, there was the drive to introduce greater specialization within the various academic fields, and new technical and scientific universities were established, thus re-enforcing and consolidating the place of sciences. The task of exploring new technological frontiers had, until then, been left to individual scholars. From this moment on, the effort became collective, leading western countries, often backed by local industries, to invest in new universities where the scientific method could flourish in purpose-built facilities, ensuring continual advances in research and innovation.

The Third Industrial Revolution, interpreted through the lens of "knowledge economy", shifted the centre of gravity from technical and scientific subjects to social sciences. Neoclassical economics and other new concepts together created the theoretical bases to sustain the process of financialization of the economy. During this phase, studies in law, economics and organizational sciences gained ground, leading to the unprecedented rise in schools of law and economics, and the proliferation of Master's in Business Administration, a model that became one of the most powerful factors homologating organizational thought across the world.

At the end of the 20th century, network technology and global connectivity flung open the doors to the Fourth Industrial Revolution. The mayhem of financial crises in 2001 and again in 2007 directed the spotlight onto the limits of models for development conceived in the second half of the 20th century. As a consequence, the escalation of social and organizational sciences within universities

DOI: 10.4324/9781003231004-01

2 Introduction

eased off, as did law and economics, and the focus turned to technical and scientific subjects. This shift was supported by the breakneck development of new high-tech sectors, spewing out "unicorns" in the digital industry which are able to inject massive investment and stoke up training and research in these sectors. The new millennium started as a phase of expansion for the major technical and scientific universities, which could spy out new opportunities and see their sphere of influence expanding within new knowledge ecosystems.

The development process in universities shone the light on their increasing impact, often at global level, in terms of steering transformation in society and economy. That said, it also emphasized their modus operandi frequently run along the lines of adapting to contingent situations driven by single research group interests, or by pronounced changes in their own ecosystem or evermore globalization in the education and training market.

Today, this tendency to be "adaptive" rather than "proactive" is having to grapple with deep social and cultural transformations, re-arrangements in geopolitical balances, environmental emergencies and frenzied technological change, all aspects spurred on also by the global Covid health crisis. In the light of this situation, loaded with many widely unexplored implications and the potential of radically upturning entire economies and societies, universities, as the driving engine of new knowledge, are enjoined to re-appraise their roles and responsibilities. We must inevitably take a long hard look at what universities intrinsically are and the models that have written their evolution. We also need to come up with the right tools to instil the strategic vision necessary to direct education and research policies that are long-lasting and can help to provide answers to the great challenges of our millennium.

In this book, we set ourselves the task of designing a manual to help technical and scientific universities navigate their way through their choices with a clearer vision and a better understanding of the impact and implications of their decisions.

The research process

This book is the outcome of the work carried out by a research group set up by the Rector of Politecnico di Milano in 2017. The brief for PoliMI 2040 was to develop a knowledge base that could be used to steer the university's long-term strategies, anticipating future scenarios and challenges, and hypothesizing potential trajectories of change.

PoliMI 2040's initial research and subsequent elaborations were geared towards analysing the ongoing macrodynamics of change and their possible repercussions on the specificity and distinctiveness of technological and scientific universities, and on these universities' current and potential role in the medium to long term.

The project was conducted by seven professors in a range of different fields, and the research process itself drew in over 300 professors, experts, researchers and research assistants at various times. Work was organized around various topics into different phases. In each phase, the procedure was to gather preliminary data and carry out a literature review, followed by discussions, interviews and round-table debates among professors and researchers, leading up to plenary sessions open to everyone in the university where we discussed and presented our intermediate findings. At the conclusion of our work, we elaborated several development settings, which we then validated through interviews and conversations with professors and researchers at other technical and scientific universities, chosen because of their status in international rankings, as well as with business experts and from the world of institutions.

The chart in Figure 0.1 shows our work model, split into two main phases and broken down by topics into thematic or focus scopes. As the chart shows, we organized our work into an initial phase, where we analysed the material qualitatively and quantitatively, and a second phase of synthetic interpretation and elaboration of models and possible settings.

In the first phase, we arranged our research into three focus scopes. In the first, we explored the broad trends currently in progress, so as to present an overview of the contexts where university systems have evolved. We were particularly keen to understand the ongoing dynamics of change determined by the shift in geopolitical balances across the globe, the impact of these dynamics on the new geographies of knowledge that are now taking shape, as well as on the current transformations within economies and societies worldwide. In parallel with analysing the

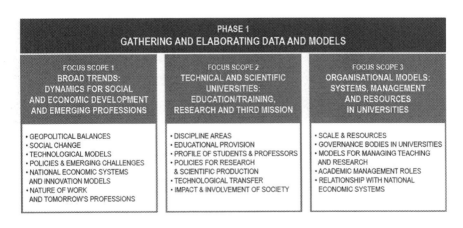

FIGURE 0.1   Project breakdown.

4 Introduction

literature, we studied international research papers and reports that shed more light on the nature of the different innovation systems in the world today, and changes in work practices and professions expected to feature prominently over the next decade or so.

In the second focus scope, we explored different university systems across the world, to gain a good understanding of their disciplines specificity, educational provision, focus of their research, and how research was advanced and promoted. We also tried to decode the profile of lecturers and students in the various universities, and how universities were able to promote themselves, their technology transfer undertakings and their social impact within their local and/or supranational systems. In this stage, we concentrated on a competitive landscape of the world's leading technical and scientific universities, identified through their position in the leading international rankings. Our data analysis and research allowed us to profile some of the universities we were examining and outline several reference models and trajectories of evolution, where we also drew on strategic planning documents published on their websites (see Table 0.1).

TABLE 0.1 Sample of technical universities grouped by geographical area

North America	Europe	Asia	Oceania
Massachusetts Institute of Technology	University of Cambridge	The University of Tokyo	The University of Melbourne
Stanford University	University of Oxford	Tokyo Institute of Technology	The University of New South Wales
Harvard University	Imperial College London	Kyoto University	Monash University
University of California, Berkeley	University College London	KAIST – Korea Advanced Institute of Science and Technology	The University of Sidney
Georgia Institute of Technology	KTH – Royal Institute of Technology	Seoul National University	Australian National University
California Institute of Technology	Technical University Denmark	Tsinghua University	
Carnegie Mellon University	Delft University of Technology	Peking University	
UCLA – University of California Los Angeles	Technical University of Munich	Zhejiang University	
Princeton University	Technical University of Berlin	Fudan University	
University of Illinois at Urbana-Champaign	RWTH Aachen University	Shanghai Jao Tong University	

North America	Europe	Asia	Oceania
University of Michigan – Ann Arbor	KIT – Kalsruhe Institute of Technology	Chinese University of Hong Kong	
University of Texas at Austin	ETH – Swiss Federal Institute of Technology	Hong Kong University of Science & Technology	
Cornell University	EPFL – École Polytechnique Fédérale de Lausanne	The University of Hong Kong	
University of Toronto	Politecnico di Milano	National Taiwan University NUS – National University of Singapore NTU – Nanyang Technological University, Singapore	

In the third focus scope, we switched our attention to the models of governance in academic organizations, to glean the interrelation between success factors and a few interesting organizational levers. We examined the overall scale, type and amount of public–private resources invested in the academic system, together with the models in place to manage teaching, research and the universities' third mission. This analysis was correlated to the relational models between universities and their institutional and legislative contexts of reference. We conducted our research by gathering data of universities in the sample, which were then supplemented by interviews with representatives from those universities selected as "archetypes" of academic governance systems.

In the second phase, associated with the fourth focus scope, we worked on consolidating and fleshing out our findings and the contributions and interpretations arising from internal and external discussions. We held several workshops which provided the material to build an interpretive model based on three axes that redefine the identity of contemporary universities, that is, the nature of knowledge produced, its system of relationships, and the organizational and governance models. We anchored several strategic guidelines to this model, each with potential settings outlining the possible impact of the different choices taken within the model's three axes. The settings developed by the work group were successively validated through discussions with representatives of the international universities and analysed in the preceding phases by experts from the worlds of business and institutions.

6 Introduction

Contents

This book consists of five chapters in which we summarize our research, examining the findings of our analysis and elaborating our interpretive models. In the conclusions, we present our process to build strategic orientation settings.

Chapter 1 explores the role of tertiary education within processes of social and economic development, and examines its outlook and impact on the main political, economic and social trends. Starting from our analysis of how university systems co-evolved with social and economic systems, in this chapter we analyse the fundamental role that these institutions play within today's "knowledge economy". This analysis examines the changes currently in progress, from the role of technology in society and the urbanization of our world to climate change and growing inequality, and identifies the responsibilities and challenges that all universities in general, and the scientific and technical institutions in particular, will be facing over the next decades.

Chapter 2 covers the spheres of action in universities, showing how past and current changes are transforming the operational boundaries of universities. In practice, what is happening is that they are branching out from their two longest-standing functions, education and research, first to include entrepreneurship innovation and, more recently, to embrace the more active role of driving awareness of technology in society and influencing policies both in the private and in the public domain. The analysis in the chapter is based upon an ideal hypothetical competitive landscape, where we selected about 20 technical and scientific universities from our initial sample, recognized internationally for their excellent performance. The comparative analysis, backed by statistical reports and theoretical insights, identifies the main trends that play an essential role in steering academic strategies in research and education, in transferring innovation to the entrepreneurial system, and on their impact and influence on society.

Chapter 3 is a critical reflection on the evolution of governance models in universities, from Humboldt's original model to the current situation where many models are in place, each having been influenced by the background conditions that determined how they evolved. This chapter first investigates the interrelations between forms of governance and the context which generated that specific arrangement, especially when juxtaposed with the various national economy development models and specific regulatory constraints. We then went down to the level of single universities, where we identified a series of archetypical models in order to summarize possible approaches to governance systems that universities can take. Starting from this analysis, and recognizing that each university is bound by national checks in the institutional, political and economic sphere, in this chapter, we trace several common trends across Europe, which are now playing a significant role in moulding university choices.

Chapter 4 outlines the directions that universities could take over the upcoming years, proposing a model which bolts the possible strategies along three axes.

Introduction 7

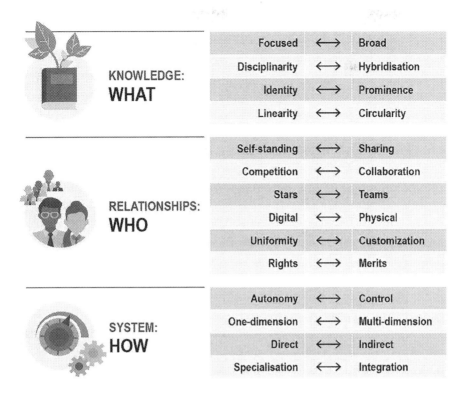

FIGURE 0.2 The 14 crossroads.

As mentioned, these axes redefine the identity of today's universities, and consist of the type and methods to create and transfer **knowledge** (*what*), the actors and their set of internal and external **relationships** (*who*), and the **system** of organizational models that govern their actions and activities (*how*). On the basis of our model, we then set out 14 crossroads that delve into the possible strategic choices that each university can make on the basis of its own objectives and the after-effects that these can determine. We identified two possible polarities for each of these 14 crossroads, with a critical discussion of the associated benefits and potential threats, in order to present well-organized arguments for or against each choice (see Figure 0.2).

Chapter 5 sets out an assessment of the prospects arising from the different choices and settings described in Chapter 4. It was possible to highlight how the various social, economic and cultural features in each context, in combination with the various institutional aspects, all contribute to shaping the array of decisions to be taken and also make one path more practical or effective under certain conditions. Under this interpretation, we are propounding a model of correlation

8 Introduction

between choices that can be made at the different crossroads. It also presents a critical interpretation of the contextual properties of each university system, giving individual universities a strategic orientation tool that can help them plan their transformation strategies in the medium to long term, while keeping a close eye on potentially imminent predicaments.

1

UNIVERSITIES AND THEIR CHALLENGES IN A CHANGING WORLD

From their inception in the Middle Ages, universities have travelled in step with the history of western societies, their changes closely mirroring the transformations in each successive era, and their models for organizing and transmitting knowledge reflecting these periods (Kerr, 1995; de Ridder-Symoens, 2003; Homer - Haskins, 2013). During the Age of Enlightenment universities took on a different form, enabling them to play a more central role in the new world of production and consumption, paraded in with the First Industrial Revolution. The concept of knowledge as a single ensemble persisted until the Renaissance and, putting aside the schools and specialist studies emerging in many fields, it embraced a pluralist vision of education, often combining humanities and sciences.[1]

This unitary approach was gradually abandoned when universities opened up to the Enlightenment, introducing hierarchies, standards and quantitative measures of productivity, all concepts belonging to the first burst of industrialization. Universities embarked upon the process of boxing knowledge into compartments, which became their mainstay throughout the 20th century. Between the late 19th century and the first quarter of the 20th century, universities replicated the model of intense specialization typical of advanced social and economic systems, along with evermore complex scientific knowledge. Programmes became more diversified, to cater for the newly institutionalized professional bodies, while competition between universities, especially in North America with its great public–private divide, led to setting further demarcation lines for the different functions of a university and a separation between teaching universities and those also capable of engaging in scientific research (Davidson, 2011).

---

1 During the Renaissance, *studia humanitatis* (the humanities), were placed at the centre of the debate on learning and knowledge, significantly influencing the progress of other subjects. See Garin E. (1996).

DOI: 10.4324/9781003231004-02

10 Universities and their challenges in a changing world

Growing economic prosperity in the West, and the ensuing increase in schooling, meant that universities could consolidate and increase their social function, a process that gained momentum from the 1950s onwards, driven by new political and institutional conditions ushered in after the Second World War. More and more students began studying for a degree in this period, albeit with differences among geographic areas. In Italy, for instance, the move to open universities to everyone with a secondary school diploma, taken in 1969, drove up the number of university students from 600,000 to over 1 million in 1979, with the numbers settling at around 1,800,000 as from 2004 (see Figures 1.1 and 1.2).

Universities, which had initially served a small circle of intellectual elite, were now accessible to wider and wider segments of society, exploiting and strengthening social and economic development. Along with many other typical western institutions, they had to take on the new millennium's deep paradigmatic crisis with a setup based on visions begotten in the Enlightenment.

1.1 Dynamics of development and evolution in universities

As western thought evolved, especially from the onset of the industrial revolutions, understanding which factors could fuel social, economic and cultural development was at the heart of the discussion (Marzano, 2008). In the first phases of human civilizations, natural resources and size of population played a critical role in determining whether they could evolve. This dynamic changed radically with the industrial revolutions and scientific and technological innovation took centre

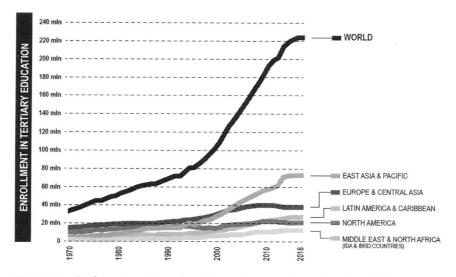

FIGURE 1.1 Students in tertiary education worldwide, time series from 1970 to 2018.
Source: The World Bank, 2020

Universities and their challenges in a changing world 11

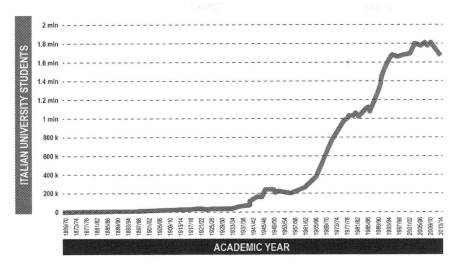

FIGURE 1.2 University students in Italy, time series from 1869 to 2014.
Source: ISTAT

place in a new development journey. Until the end of the 18th century, 70% of the world's economy was concentrated in Asia, where economic development was more or less based on agriculture and depended on access to land resources. China and India, the two countries with the largest populations in the world, dominated the scene, including economically (Figure 1.3).

The philosophical roots of western culture, the way reality was represented and how knowledge was classified and transmitted, contained the premises for instigating a paradigmatic transformation. Two key ingredients in this journey were the continuous development of European universities, which had already begun in the Middle Ages, and the later drive to reorganize their disciplinary approach and knowledge during the Enlightenment. Between the late 18th and mid-20th centuries, this journey culminated in the First and Second Industrial Revolutions, unveiling the effects of thought and scientific method when applied to transforming the real world (Cohen, 1994; Detti & Gozzini, 2009).

First the steam engine, then electricity and petroleum derivatives upturned productivity levels in production processes and sparked off an economic growth no longer dependent on size of population or natural resources, giving Europe, North America and Japan headway in economic leadership at global level. Unsurprisingly, the start of the Second Industrial Revolution was the trigger in all main western countries to invest in building universities and research centres specializing in technical and scientific subjects.[2] The vision underpinning this process is clear: do

2 École Polytechnique in Paris – 1794, TU Delft – 1842, ETH in Zurich – 1855, EPFL in Lausanne – 1853, MIT in Boston – 1861, Tokyo University of Science – 1881, Stanford University in San Francisco – 1885, Caltech in Pasadena – 1891.

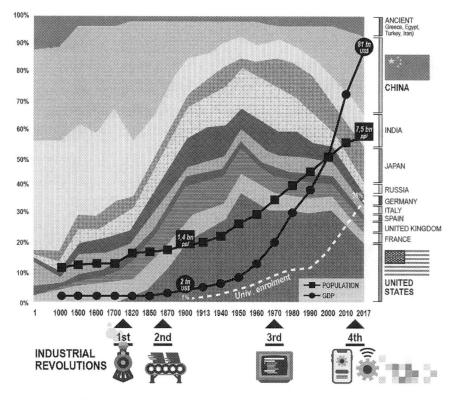

FIGURE 1.3   Global dynamics.

Source: The World Bank (2019) and International Monetary Fund (2019)

not relegate technological innovation to individual and occasionally serendipitous discovery. Instead, establish places with consolidated research practice, which are interwoven into the industrial and productive fabric, in turn often involved in the financing side.

The massive acceleration imparted to development by the creation of interconnected systems of actors involved in education, research and innovation was further accentuated by the dynamics of globalization. In terms of cultural and social hybridization and ecosystems transformation, the globalization process cementing the Anthropocene Epoch was certainly rooted much further back. Nevertheless, it was with the Second and, above all, the Third Industrial Revolution that the quickening in global flows of goods, people, financial resources and knowledge had such deep impact on the relationship between geographic areas and regional economic systems (Mann, 2011; McNeill & Engelke, 2014). Until the mid-20th century, the ability to elaborate and apply technical and scientific innovations to production processes and economic systems was firmly in the hands of the western world, Europe and North America, plus Japan (Lacaita, 1973). There was a radical change of direction in economic and social development, and to the conditions of life in these areas.

By the mid-20th century, after nearly 200 years of technological and industrial advancements, 80% of the world's economy was concentrated in the West. Economic growth and improved life conditions initiated a slow process of growth in population and level of schooling, even leading, as we have mentioned, to an increase in the number of people studying at universities. The subsequent expansion in universities and their growing influence had, in turn, a decisive impact in directing the economic and social policies that shaped the second half of the 20th century.

The Third Industrial Revolution injected further acceleration to the transformation of western economies, through more extensive automation and by tapping into the potential of elaborating computer information. Information technology opened the doors to globalized knowledge, and this proceeded hand in hand with unprecedented advances in social sciences within university studies, especially economic science. This transformation has been analysed in several studies, highlighting the fact that, in 1920, social sciences had been taught in only 11% of countries, climbing to 60% by 1980, mainly at the expense of human sciences in the strictest sense and studies in classic and local culture (Wong, 1991; Frank & Gabler, 2006). Neoclassic economic theory in the late 19th century had already sparked a process to transfer traditional basic science models, applied in mathematics and physics, to economic and social subjects. Additionally, from the mid-20th century onwards, the theory of endogenous growth stated that technological innovation should be interpreted as the key factor in driving the dynamics of progress (Grilli, 2005). The development of financial capitalism during the Third Industrial Revolution took shape on the wave of these perceptions, strongly backed by financialization models claimed to be scientifically sound and by the processing power of computer technology (Piketty, 2013).

This is when schools of economics reached their peak internationally, the centre of gravity of the university system (and the economy) moved from Europe to the United States, and post-degree education was galvanized by the surge in MBAs, in particular.[3] In the United States alone, the number of students taking MBAs soared by 400% between mid-20th century and the first decade of the next, with a decisive impact on all education systems globally. The basic concept underpinning this massive uptake was the progressive assimilation of organization and management theories to scientific theories, with the social dimension of economics being gradually abandoned and the focus turning mainly to financial aspects (Baker, 2014).

---

3 From the first business school, the École Supérieure de Commerce de Paris (ESCP), founded in 1819 and, in the United States, the first collegiate business school, the Wharton School at the University of Pennsylvania, established in 1881 (with the first Master's in Business Administration), to the thresholds of the 21st century, over 1,000 business schools have been established across the world, with more than 2,000 MBA courses. But the true upsurge in enrolments came in the second half of the 20th century. See Baker D. (2014), *The schooled society*, Stanford University Press, Stanford.

14 Universities and their challenges in a changing world

At the end of the 20th century, while the financial system expanded to absorb graduates within economic and legal spheres, and often found new application fields where physics and mathematics could be put to good use, technical subjects felt the effect of manufacturing industries relocating to developing countries. The surplus of highly qualified graduates in technical subjects, often with doctorates, from the great American scientific and technical universities, combined with the new world entrepreneurial spirit, was probably a significant factor in lighting the flame of the Fourth Industrial Revolution, which took about half the time to appear than on previous occasions.

Network technology and worldwide connections inject new power to the global flows of finance, goods, services, knowledge and people, determining an unprecedented overall economic and social growth (joined, as we will see, by increasing imbalances and inequalities), which is reflected in the rise of the level of schooling on a worldwide scale. Today, 38% of young people between 18 and 25 are in tertiary education (The World Bank, 2020). However, the outcome of this final development phase is highly controversial and opens new challenges to universities, especially because of three conditions that put past models into disarray.

In the first place, the type of technology implicated in the Fourth Industrial Revolution is, in many respects, a paradigm leap whose effects are largely unexplored. For one thing, network technologies are eating away at the boundaries between physical and virtual reality (*Internet of People* and *Internet of Things*), radically altering the practices of communication and interaction, and the processes of producing and utilizing goods, services and information (e.g. *sharing economy, distributed manufacturing*). These changes speed up the obsolescence of scientific and technological knowledge, and carry with them, as in any technological leap, the risk of inflicting negative effects on work and jobs. Highly efficient networks with extensive coverage (5G), the power of elaboration achieved and the new forms of artificial intelligence have made it increasingly more difficult, if not impossible, to foresee the medium- and long-term effects of applying these technologies.

While access to information and knowledge is apparently on the rise, so are the distortion effects that affect both those who can access digital technology and those who cannot. The ones who have this access are experiencing limitations to the protection of their personal data, with new mechanisms to control information imposed by the technological giants. The ones who have nots see the digital divide growing and are basically excluded from the networks where knowledge circulates and value is generated (Morozov, 2016). Finally, we are witnessing the convergence of different scientific and technological domains, where organic and inorganic sciences are merging, and mechanical and computer technology are hybridizing with life sciences, raising serious questions on the ethical front and that of social impact (Roco et al., 2013).

In the second place, the rippling effects determined by the financial system becoming progressively detached from the real economy, which initiated and then accelerated in the mid-20th century, cannot easily be traced back to the positive visions elaborated in that period. The crises in the financial markets, which emerged

Universities and their challenges in a changing world **15**

in the United States first in 2000 and again in 2007 and rebounded throughout the western world, put the spotlight on the limits of economic and development models drawn up in the second half of the 20th century (Galimberti, 2002; Gallino, 2011). The economic policies inspired by these models and set up to oppose such crises had, in turn, social implications that were often dramatic and which ultimately inflicted recessive effects on western economies, especially in Europe.

This was followed by a gradual contraction in the economic cycle that accentuated the competition between local and national economic systems, set against declining resources. Among the main distortion effects were an increase in social inequality between the "ruling classes" and everyone else, and a first-time drop in middle-class income, countered by the continuous global growth in the assets of the very wealthy, conditions that are creating a climate of weariness and mistrust towards the institutions that had guided the previous century.[4] This situation has also undermined state coffers, especially in Europe, with countries gradually reducing public spending, above all on education (with repercussions on universities), social policies and health, albeit with differences from country to country (Stiglitz, 2015, 2018).

The third critical condition concerns the transition between the Third and Fourth Industrial Revolutions, where globalization processes once again changed the world's balance. Immediately after western manufacturing began being relocated to Asian countries, China especially embarked on its own path of scientific and technological innovation. This campaign was mounted by gaining access to technology in the hands of western investors and ceded in return for various kinds of benefits for their own economic and production ventures in China. In a very short time, the Chinese industrial, research and education systems had achieved levels of competitiveness equivalent to those in the western world, enabled by the particularly agile political and institutional conditions linked to "market socialism" (Chow & Perkins, 2015). The effect of this process is that Asia now accounts for over 50% of the global economy, with growth rates still far above those of other economies and a rising and controversial place in global geopolitical balance, where the pertinacious antagonism between the United States and China is prefiguring totally different scripts than in any preceding phase (Feldman, 2013; Colombo & Magri, 2020).

New geographies of knowledge and new production systems are cropping up around the world, accentuating the creation of highly attractive regions and others in recession, in a model centred on large metropolitan areas in strong competition with each other. National policies struggle to restore balance, and political instability generates new social pressure from regions exposed to conflict and environmental emergency. New geopolitical equilibriums are also influenced by the effects of the deepening environmental and global warming crises, with their unexpected

---

4 From 1980 to today, the richest 1% of the population has increased its income by 240%, lifting its percentage of overall income from 10% to 21%, while the income for 90% of the population has remained more or less the same. See Milanovic (2016), Piketty (*op. cit*).

16 Universities and their challenges in a changing world

impacts on the flow of migration, opening the doors to major challenges in sustainability, including on the social front (Khanna, 2016; Latour, 2018).

The combination of the three conditions mentioned earlier has recently hindered the rise in social and economic sciences within universities, focusing attention overwhelmingly on those geared towards sciences and technology. The blistering crisis that originated in the financial economy, compounded by the rise of "unicorns" in the digital sector, has generated renewed interest in innovation within technology and driven the demand for both education and investment in research. Technical universities have, thus, entered a new phase of expansion, which, in turn, is packed with many questions and new challenges.

First of all, as we have said, technology in its 4.0 incarnations can change the way we work and significantly influence production models and development dynamics across the world more radically than in the past industrial revolutions. Digital technology certainly plays its part, but it is not alone, as we only have to think of nanotechnology, genomics and all the fields involved in the current technological convergence. This expansion demands, especially from technical and scientific universities, the ability to keep up with the ongoing changes, understanding them, and updating knowledge and skills, so that the processes of education will be able to respond to a world of work that will be totally transformed when it emerges from the transition phase.

In second place, we are now fully aware of the limits of neoclassical economics theory, with its linear interpretation, whereby technological innovation stimulates economic growth, economic growth creates the premises for prosperity within the population, the population increases its level of schooling and learns the skills needed to promote and manage technological innovation. On this point, it is really up to the technical universities to acknowledge and embrace their place in complex ecosystems of innovation and research, and be able to redraw their relationship with public and private stakeholders and with civil society.

Finally, the current climate of instability in geopolitical balance, and the emergence of new innovation systems around the world, place technology at the centre of a highly competitive landscape. And so, technical and scientific universities must know how to elaborate strategies to guide and direct education and research, deploying their ever-greater capacity to evaluate the effects of their education and research on society, culture and the environment, and even recapturing and strengthening a humanistic and pluralistic vision of scientific culture.

1.2 Work, skills and education in the knowledge society

Starting in the mid-1960s and helped by the growing widespread access to tertiary education, economic and social sciences instigated new considerations about the impact of the various production factors on the processes of development and innovation, centring the debate on intangible factors, human resources and knowledge. The acceleration in transformation processes caused by the Third Industrial Revolution and the uptake of digital technologies triggered the re-elaboration of theories that saw technological innovation as the main motor of development, heralding modern companies into the "knowledge economy" (Quinn, 1992; Solow, 2000; Grilli, 2005; Marzano, 2008).

The "knowledge economy" brings with it radical changes to the nature of work, which are reflected in the form assumed by organizations. Vertical hierarchical structures focused on specialized functions and processes that follow one another in a linear sequence are slowly being reshaped along horizontal lines, organized into parallel processes, and arranged by projects that bring together a range of functions and skills (Crozier, 1989; Butera et al., 1997).

Changes in the nature of technology, arising from processes of miniaturization and its application into increasing multi-disciplinary fields, together with the proliferation of actors who can generate and spread innovation, are redesigning the boundaries of companies, organizations and professions.

We are no longer dealing with closed entities, but bodies inserted seamlessly within new systems of relationships and collaborative networks, under the banner of "open innovation" (Normann & Ramirez, 1993; Chesbrough, 2003).

With the advent of net-based technologies and the potential given by integrating and connecting real and virtual realities (Internet of Things, Artificial Intelligence), the Fourth Industrial Revolution has set new challenges to the workplace in transformation and the skillset now needed. Different from previous technological paradigms, this metamorphosis rolled up in half the time, bringing home the impossibility for contemporary social and economic systems to base professional development and training on the generational changeover. The current transformation has paved the way to serious considerations on its impact on employment, the profiles that will be needed in the near future and, finally, on continuous professional development, now a must throughout a person's professional life. Since the Luddites in the 19th century, all main technological advancements have been met with increasing and widespread apprehension and diffidence ever, but the rapid pace of the ongoing changes calls for a even more careful examination.

In a famous study two Oxford researchers, Carl Frey and Michael Osborne (2013, resumed and expanded 2015), examined how susceptible jobs are to computerization, looking at 702 job profiles in the United States. According to their study, 47% of the total American employment is at risk of computerization and could be replaced by a machine within, they estimated, one or two decades. These results were substantially confirmed in subsequent studies (McKinsey & Co., 2017), where it emerged that at least 30% of tasks could be automated in 60% of current functions, and by 2030 between 75 and 375 million workers (3% to 14% of the global workforce) will be forced to change the type of job, and they will all need to evolve to factor in the changes deriving from the arrival of new technology.

Looking at the past, it is nothing new. As an example of unstable times analysed by historians, the current crisis seems to mirror the havoc that took place in Europe within the period referred to as the Crisis of the 14th Century (or Crisis of the Late Middle Ages), which paved the way to the Renaissance (Kline Cohn, 2008; Barbero, 2019). And what about the sense of loss that J. M. Keynes (1963) highlighted amidst the Great Depression of the 1930s, or the fear in the 1960s about the possible effects of the first automated industrial processes?

If we analyse the past, we generally find confirmation that, when new technologies are implemented, the people whose jobs were replaced by new solutions and automated processes are excluded from the workplace in the short term. Nevertheless, the longer-term effects are positive, leading to a surge in demand for new employment and a global change in productivity, with work hours dropping as a consequence (the average workweek, part of worker demands since at least the late 19th century, is about 50% less than in the early 1900s within advanced economies, the outcome of a shorter working day, more holidays and the recent expansion of part-time working). The authors of the various studies all agree that jobs and professional positions are less likely to become obsolescent when they involve: i) a high level of creativity (in the arts, sciences and engineering) and manual dexterity (creative professions), ii) a significant dose of "ethical and social intelligence" (e.g. education and healthcare) and iii) the need to manage unexpected events (managing emergencies). In general, across salary levels or the various geopolitical development models, the risk of being replaced is not uniform.

In advanced economies, there is less risk attached to high profile professions, defined by upper levels of education and income. Tertiary education is thus emerging as one of the most strategic levers to ensure professional stability since it can match the transformation in skills and work required in the near future. In recent studies, changes to professions are seen as a major driver of demographic and socio-economic change (Figure 1.4) and the new technologies for managing data are considered the most significant element of technological change (Figure 1.5).

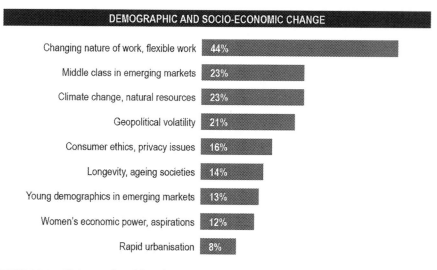

FIGURE 1.4 Drivers of social and economic change.

Source: The Future of Jobs, World Economic Forum (2016)

Universities and their challenges in a changing world 19

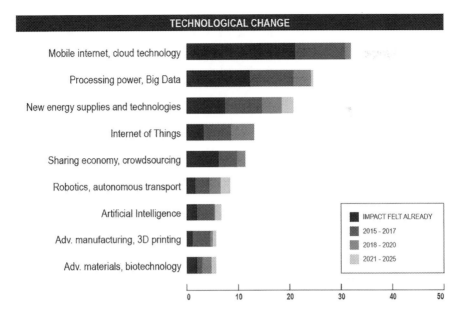

FIGURE 1.5 Drivers of technological change.
Source: The Future of Jobs, World Economic Forum (2016)

If we analyse the type of skills that will be in demand over the next years (presented in Figure 1.6), the picture clearly shows an increased request for cognitive ability, and knowing how to take a systemic view and solve complex problems, while there will be lesser demand for specific technical skills or outstanding physical prowess. In brief, the idea gaining ground is that we must pass on the capacity to learn how to learn, more than transferring knowledge and skills that will soon become obsolete.

Building up cognitive skills rather than focusing on specific technical knowledge goes some way towards explaining why it is impossible to entrust skill renewal to generational changeover. This position has become ingrained within advanced economies, where continuous training is now a strategic element and a must. The process of adapting to technological change by merely replacing people ("hiring and firing") is no longer feasible; with the current rate of change to technology, it would translate into a 9- to 18-month staff turnover. Learning while doing is another crucial element in continuous learning because the model of change included in corporate strategies no longer allows the various phases of planning and implementation to be carried out in sequence (Edmondson & Saxberg, 2017). The need for continuous learning and updating of skills is very much linked to the form of contemporary organizations. Their transformation has been induced by exogenous changes (globalization, economic crises, re-arrangement of geopolitical balances), and also by theories underpinning the establishment of leaner organizations, where the various functions come with greater responsibility, professional figures are more autonomous, and they have wider and more complex duties within collaborative work groups (Rullani, 2004; Bonazzi, 2008).

Career paths are also changing and unlikely to proceed completely within a single organization, being instead inserted in elaborate multi-structured networks. This framework is altering the very nature of work and, even when it evolves within a company, it takes on features traditionally associated with self-employed professional work, where roles are less stringently coded, and skills must be constantly reconfigured and updated to match the different settings. As well as collaborating with other units in an organization, people must also work closely with their professional community of reference (see Figure 1.6).

In this field, while looking back to the past can be somehow reassuring, the current historical moment is totally unique because of the speed and sweeping nature of ongoing change, and it requires prompt, precise answers. This is the area where universities are taking on an impressive and valuable role. First of all, they must become interpreters of the ongoing changes to knowledge and learning, reflecting and anticipating the type of skills and profiles required in the near future. Secondly, they must embed continuous learning at the core of their mission to educate. This

FIGURE 1.6 Changes to core competencies demanded by the job market 2015–2020.

Source: The Future of Jobs, World Economic Forum (2016)

Universities and their challenges in a changing world **21**

factor emerges as one of the strategic priorities upholding the development of modern companies, and it highlights the necessity to redefine the entire relationship between universities, professions and institutions.

1.3 National economies, local hubs and models of research and innovation

While the impact of technological innovation on the nature of work is certainly the main challenge, we must also gain a clear understanding of the role now taken by universities in research and technological transfer within local development dynamics. From the second half of the 20th century onwards, we have witnessed a change to global balances in terms of capacity for growth and development, with the specific features being determined by the scale of the systems in place, be it in continents, countries or metropolitan areas.

At the continental scale, as we have said, the centre of gravity has moved towards Asian countries, given that North America has recently been reaping only modest economic growth, driven mainly by the financial sector and fuelled by the boom of IT companies (share of GDP up by 32% in ten years), and by demographic stability, where the outcome is an ageing population. Europe's development is similar to North America's with regard to population, but its innovation and economic growth is less pronounced (share of GDP up by 18% in ten years). Asia, on the other hand, still enjoys sustained economic growth driven by significant industrial investment (up by 300% in ten years), with its population projected to increase until the second half of this century. Africa is still to develop economically and will account for most of the world's growth in population over the next century, with migration pressure remaining strong especially towards Europe, in part driven by continuous environmental crises (United Nations, 2019).

Technological innovation has played a crucial part in this re-balancing process, seen as the main engine of economic development, a role highlighted by the growing weight of investment in research and development. Until the last century, North America was the primary global investor in R&D, followed by Europe. In recent years, total annual R&D investment rose to over 2.3 trillion dollars, but today 44% of this investment is in Asia, against 28% in North America and 21% in Europe (R&D Magazine, 2019). This inversion in the trend of R&D investment is reflected in the positioning of technical universities. Asian universities are now climbing up the rankings, outvying those in America and, albeit only partially for now, those in Europe (see Figure 1.7).

Within the various continental areas, the models to support innovation and technological transfer often vary from country to country. The policies in each country can be seen in Figure 1.8, alongside the resources invested (input) and the results obtained (output). Among the inputs are, for instance, public spending on R&D funded by public and/or private finances, private spending on R&D, and financial tools available for investing in innovation, such as venture capital funds. These investments can be connected to results obtained (output) in a number

22 Universities and their challenges in a changing world

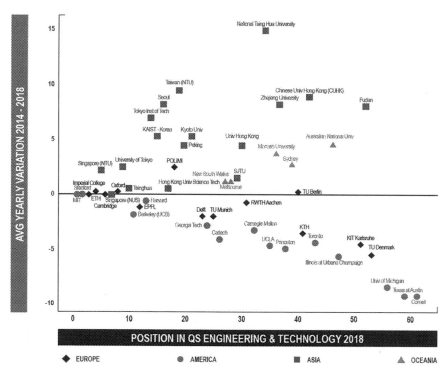

FIGURE 1.7 Positioning dynamics of the main technical universities.

Source: Analysis based on 2019 QS Rankings

of scientific publications, a number of patents lodged by universities and public research centres and lodged overall, percentage of adults with a degree, and percentage of people working in technological and scientific sectors.

If we analyse several of the most representative OECD countries, we can extrapolate three quite different development models (Figure 1.8). The first model is based on a strategy to advance research and includes countries that invest extraordinary sums in R&D, well above the OECD average. These resources come from both private and public purses and generate a virtuous cycle involving public actors, private actors, and research centres and universities (we often refer to the "triple helix" model of university-industry-government relations). Countries engaging in this three-fold interaction generally deliver good results in terms of innovation and level of education.

The second model is closely focused on results and the benefits of research, and includes countries where R&D investments are basically within the OECD average and can be skewered towards the public or the private sector at any one time. This kind of investment is apparently more effective than in the previous model, meaning that these countries can deliver good results in innovation and education.

Universities and their challenges in a changing world   23

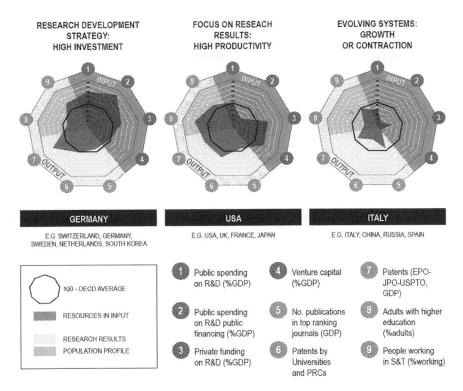

FIGURE 1.8   Position of several countries against the OECD average.
Source: Adapted from Gherardini (2015)

The third and last model contains a rather wide set of systems in evolution, and the evolution can go either way, with a clear growth in innovation in some countries, while others are in contraction. The first subset includes countries that are investing heavily in R&D and, while the results are yet to meet the OECD average for innovation and level of education, they are on a rapid upward curve (e.g. China). The second subset relates to countries that are still coming up with fairly satisfactory results in levels of innovation and education notwithstanding their minimum investment in R&D (e.g. Italy). In many cases, these are countries that are coasting, living off the benefits of a long period of past growth, but which risk rapid decline if they do not embark upon a new virtuous path of research and innovation.

While Europe encompasses a range of diverse situations, as a whole it is in line with the OECD average, except for the smaller presence of venture capital funds to invest in innovation and fewer graduates, although more patents are lodged, especially in Germany and the Nordic countries. This is decidedly not enough for a geographic area that had been able to guide some of the past industrial revolutions.

24 Universities and their challenges in a changing world

If Europe wants to play an important part in future social and economic development, it must invest more in R&D than the OECD average and become a credible player that can hold its own against North America and Asia. If the next revolution implies directing research and technology towards new paradigms of social, cultural and environmental sustainability, Europe has already shown that it can take on a leadership role in this arena. Increased investment in research and innovation could consolidate and strengthen its identity, which could become an element of equilibrium in the playing fields of competitive intercontinental dynamics.

However, the complexity of these forces cannot be grasped if we only look at continents and national economies. We must also analyse metropolitan regions, and examine the role that cities play in promoting the processes of development (Acs, 2004; Agnoletti et al., 2014; Sugrue, 2014). Even the large metropolitan systems, with their extensive networks and global connections, mirror the ongoing transformation in global balances, and the polarization typical of today's world between areas that are becoming more attractive and areas that are in decline (Secchi, 2013; Governa, 2015). In particular, the economic, social and knowledge ecosystems gradually being created are clearly determining the direction of development in universities and their strategic choices.

Universities are closely intertwined with the local systems that generate and disseminate knowledge, and consist of the businesses, organizations and public authorities operating in the local area. When all the actors, including the universities, come together in a virtuous and dynamic interplay, this stimulates the development of knowledge and also of the local area, contributing towards strengthening the link between economic and social prosperity. The universities inserted in these great metropolitan regions become pivotal hubs between local and global knowledge networks, and can draw in the best human capital because they are integrated within vibrant and attractive ecosystems that invest in the university system (Etzkowitz & Leydesdorff, 2000; Moretti, 2012).

The emblematic cases (see Figure 1.9) are in California, along the Boston–New York East Coast axis and in Asia's emerging areas (Hong Kong, Singapore, Shanghai and Tokyo). In Europe, London remains an attractive hub, although the effects of Brexit are a great unknown, while the Germany–Switzerland axis is a stable and dominant presence, and there is interest in the evolving areas of Paris and Northern Europe (Sassen, 1991). In Italy, the only area with features similar to those described is the Milan metropolitan region, although there are serious limitations that derive from the country's economic outlook compared to its European competitors. Also, we still have to see how the local manufacturing systems will evolve. In the past, they had played a major role in Italy's development, but today's transformation is hampered by their inability to mould themselves into ecosystems based on knowledge, where universities can have a central role (Becattini, 1989; Cainelli & Zoboli, 2004).

In the setting described, understanding the new forms of creating and propagating knowledge and innovation must be a key factor in steering research strategies within universities, and in shaping their relationships with the broader system

FIGURE 1.9 Top 50 university cities by QS Ranking 2019.

of public and private actors, nationally and internationally. Recent history has highlighted how important universities are, especially technical and scientific universities, for social and cultural development, alongside their established role in economic growth and in business. It also points out the limits of purely competitive strategies, those fuelling the economic and social divide between communities, regions and national economic systems.

1.4 Current trends and today's challenges for universities

The trends described in the previous pages are transforming the very core of professions and skills that will be needed in the future. They are also changing the geography of knowledge in a landscape where competition between university systems is advancing. The role of universities is likewise changing, often against a backdrop of progressively less funds to invest in policies linked to teaching, research and innovation. This situation demands careful thought about the possible impact that these various dynamics may have on what a university actually is and on the challenges that these changes entail for the future of these icons of learning and knowledge.

In the first place, the speed of technological innovation is pushing the accelerator of change, a factor especially evident in genetics, neuroscience, biotechnology, artificial intelligence and IT, and is producing unforeseen effects whose future impact is a totally closed book (Roco et al., 2013). This issue, especially, beyond the obvious implications for teaching arrangements in universities, can impact the actual ways in which we access and transfer knowledge. Technological evolution

26 Universities and their challenges in a changing world

has come into its own with distance learning, implemented by universities across the world to cope with the Covid-19 pandemic. It could now help in the drive towards democratization and diffusion of knowledge, as well as in the sphere of teaching and research, despite there also being contrary visions and signposts pointing the other way (Rifkin, 2000; Sundararajan, 2016). We can see that, in a world criss-crossed by global networks of information, the dynamics of creating new knowledge often elude the processes and places formally appointed for this purpose, such as universities, research centres and R&D hubs. Today's mature debate on open innovation is sending out its own signals on this point, while in academia, the ever-increasing number of shared data resources now available could easily become out of reach for single institutions to manage on their own (Chesbrough, 2003; Hansen & Birkinshaw, 2006).

There is a parallel growth of interest in the open publishing model, fuelled and used by a community steadily replenished by scholars and researchers, within and without academic circles. This aspect could make its mark on the dynamics of producing and circulating knowledge, away from traditional formal frameworks, and even question the very model of universities (Bernius, 2013). Examining the processes of teaching and learning, the spreading of digital models, in the form of MOOCs and SPOCs, in particular after the Covid-19 crisis, has opened the doors to education becoming understood as a continuous process, which every person adapts to their own needs and that extends throughout their life. This situation raises two key points for the university system overall. Firstly, there is the need to develop selective and critical skills to verify the trustworthiness of information emanating from this "grey area" of knowledge, with its often unknown levels of authenticity and certification. Secondly, university campuses could learn to see themselves in a different light and less as places appointed to create and transmit knowledge in a one-directional and exclusive process. Their attractiveness could in future depend on their ability to offer true added value to researchers and scholars, in that they would be places for social meetings, for experimentation and for creative and collaborative work (with advanced research facilities, testing spaces, FabLabs, etc.). Trials of various kinds are being held in the United States and Asia, while the European university system appears to be more conservative, and cautious about change, also because it is often anchored to public policies that can ensure high standards in quality, but also tend to create uniformity in solutions and models used by individual institutions (Curaj et al., 2015; Carey, 2016).

In the second place, shrinking finances for education and research in many regions across the world, particularly in Europe, are producing negative, often distorted, effects on the university system. To start with, there is the widespread need to access external funding over and above funds received from the regional and national public purse. Apart from a few virtuous examples in central and northern Europe, like Germany, the Netherlands and some Scandinavian countries, where governments have continued to support universities with coherent public investment, university fees in many other places have been raised and finances sought through research contracts with third parties. In the United Kingdom, for example, university fees have gone up conspicuously in all universities (Triventi, 2012). While producing inequality in the right to study (the subject of policies historically wielded more solidly in Europe than elsewhere), this process can also engender medium to long-term negative effects on the nature and impact of scientific research. The reliance on non-public funding tends to limit university independence and reduce their capacity to invest in core research, since third-party funders are more interested in paying for projects on applied research.

In many cases, including research projects selected on competitive bases, even the sources of public funding are facing an increase in constraints introduced to direct universities towards areas with greater and more immediate impact on the economy.[5] Alongside the possible fallouts mentioned, many universities facing a loss of resources have justifiably tried to implement more efficient management processes tailored to their student numbers and workload, to make better use of resources available.

The introduction of the *new public management* model, designed to improve efficiency in public service organizations, was intended to make the running of universities more "business-like" with greater controls. It also often created a greater separation between the roles and functions held by the academic body and the administrative and management side. This change certainly created a more efficient system, with simplified decision-making processes. It also eliminated the functions of several collegiate bodies, thereby reducing people's motivation and deterring them from taking an active part in university life, underwhelmed by short-term efficiency criteria. In Italy and other countries, the political will to give universities their independence also introduced control mechanisms at a distance, with the ensuing significant intrusion of national policies and a strain on university administration and the management of faculty and staff. The additional bureaucratic procedures curtailed the room for experimentation even further, along with people's freedom to take initiatives. All the work to implement the complex European regulatory framework (credit system, type and classes of degrees, subject areas, etc.) also slowed down and weighed on all updating to courses and programmes, where it is difficult to try out new ideas that may have to be reversed or put new teaching concepts into action. Think of the legislative mechanisms at play in Italy, for example, which can explain the breadth of this undertaking in Italian universities: classes of degrees and degree accreditation come under national law, and subjects are pigeon-holed into classes at the central level, with these classes setting the rules for the courses proposed.

Additionally, the current size of academic bodies everywhere, the decision to yoke them to public policies, and the social and civic role of these policies have driven governments to anchor university financing to indicators and parameters that can be measured and justified clearly. This position has often pushed aside wide-ranging education and research policies grounded in strategic objectives

---

5 These constraints are particularly evident in European policies and are mirrored in plans supporting research from the "Seventh Framework Programme" to "Horizon 2020".

28 Universities and their challenges in a changing world

rather than on processes geared towards evaluating past performance. As of today, these parameters basically consist of a clutch of bibliometric indicators, now used internationally, to measure the production of scientific articles and their impact on the scientific community, linked to the reputation of the place where the article was published and the number of citations. Universities have started to concentrate on optimizing these indicators, directing their efforts towards publishing articles as if this were the main purpose of the research. On the one hand, the balance between teaching and research can be at risk, side-lining teaching, in that it is less closely tied up in the dynamics of acquiring resources. On the other, the nature of research itself may become distorted when the prospect of publishing in the short term is in conflict with processes targeting radical innovation only loosely connected to the various indicators, at least in the short time span allotted to university analyses.

Finally, in what apparently goes countercurrent to new technology that enables greater access to knowledge and the democratization of university education, populist movements are being stoked up across the world, often taking on the semblances of neo-nationalism. These movements, sometimes bound up in anachronistic ideology in their stance towards the results of scientific and technological development, could potentially restrict the circulation of information and curb international debate and the university world as we know it (De Martin, 2016). This trend is sometimes connected to economic crisis and worsening lifestyle; other times, it is anchored to cultural and social models traditionally based on cultural and economic protectionism. In either case, it is forging ahead across wide geographical regions. In Italy and elsewhere, it is often joined by increasing scepticism towards the university world, seen as detached and unable to give tangible answers to the need for skills that can be hawked in the job market. The extreme fragmentation of Italy's economic and industrial system, its high levels of deep-rooted underfunding, and the totally different social and economic landscapes from region to region mean that it is difficult to set up "one size fits all" policies and solutions. These features strengthen simplistic and forced visions that tend to fuel the delegitimization of universities, sometimes to justify the fact that public spending is being directed towards other sectors in national policies, at a time when resources are particularly scarce (Viesti, 2016).

In this setting, the pressing need in universities is to elaborate models and strategies to oppose this trend, acting decisively to underline their role in society and pointing out all the factors of excellence that define so many universities in Italy, as flagged up by a series of indicators. First of all, Italian graduates and PhD researchers are warmly received in leading international universities, endorsing a system that produces an average level of quality that is higher than, say, in the United Kingdom or the United States, where there are substantial differences between the group of excellent universities and the others. This process of re-legitimization can begin by getting across the clear message of the cultural, scientific and civic value generated by educating students and through research, and the positive effects of research on the country's overall economy and production system in the short, medium and long term. Finally, universities must recognize the importance of taking an active and responsible role to deal with the great global challenges of today, where the scale and complexity of the forces at play require additional effort by all actors in the system and especially in academia, being uniquely placed to elaborate new ideas and solutions.

As described, the actual or potential impact of these ongoing changes on the university world is configuring new settings in education and research. Against this backdrop, technical universities are emerging as the key actors, and are called upon first to interpret and elaborate knowledge, models and solutions to tackle future challenges. However, the renewed emphasis on technical and scientific culture raises further questions about the universities' capacity to steer their own education and research policies, and also about the potential strategies to build new networks of connections between a wider pool of players. The end game for these universities is to play a more active and responsible part in promoting the dynamics of global development focused on sustainability and a fairer society.

Chapter references

Acs, Z. J. (2004). Innovation and the growth of cities. *Contributions to Economic Analysis, 266,* 635–658. https://doi.org/10.1016/S0573-8555(04)66020-2

Agnoletti, C., Camagni R., Iommi S., & Lattarulo P. (Eds.). (2014). *Competitività urbana e policentrismo in Europa. Quale ruolo per le città metropolitane e le città medie.* Bologna: Il Mulino.

Baker, D. (2014). *The schooled society.* Stanford, CA: Stanford University Press.

Barbero, A. (2019). *Crisi e rivoluzione – 1348. La peste nera e la crisi del Trecento: Lezioni di Storia* (Audio book). Bari: Laterza.

Becattini, G. (1989). *Modelli locali di sviluppo.* Bologna: Il Mulino.

Bernius, S. (2013). The impact of open access on the management of scientific knowledge. *Online Information Review, 34*(4). www.emeraldinsight.com/doi/full/10.1108/14684521011072990

Bonazzi, G. (2008). *Storia del pensiero organizzativo.* Milano, Italy: Franco Angeli.

Butera, F., Donati, E., & Cesaria, R. (1997). *I lavoratori della conoscenza.* Milano, Italy: Franco Angeli.

Cainelli, G., & Zoboli, R. (2004). *The evolution of industrial districts, changing governance, innovation and internationalization of local capitalism in Italy.* Berlin, Germany: Springer.

Carey, K. (2016). *The end of college: Creating the future of learning and the university of everywhere.* New York, NY: Riverhead Books.

Chesbrough, H. W. (2003). *Open innovation: The new imperative for creating and profiting from technology.* Boston, MA: Harvard Business Press.

Chow, G. C., & Perkins, D. H. (2015). *Routledge handbook of the Chinese economy.* London: Routledge.

Cohen, H. F. (1994). *The scientific revolution: A historiographical inquiry.* Chicago, IL: University of Chicago Press.

Colombo, A., & Magri, P. (Eds.). (2020). *La fine di un mondo, atto II.* Milano, Italy: LediPublishing.

Crozier, M. (1989). *L'entreprise a' l'écoute: Apprendre le management post-industriel.* Paris, France: InterÉditions.

30 Universities and their challenges in a changing world

Curaj, A., Matei L., Pricopie R., Salmi J., & Scott P. (2015). *The European higher education area between critical reflections and future policies.* Berlin, Germany: Springer.

Davidson, C. (2011). *Now you see it: How technology and brain science will transform the way we live, work, and learn.* New York, NY: Penguin Books.

De Martin, J. C. (2016). *Università futura: Tra democrazia e bit.* Torino, Italy: Codice Edizioni.

de Ridder-Symoens, H. (2003). *A history of the university in Europe.* Cambridge: Cambridge University Press.

Detti, T., & Gozzini, G. (Ed.). (2009). *La Rivoluzione industriale tra l'Europa e il mondo.* Milano, Italy: Bruno Mondadori.

Edmondson, A., & Saxberg, B. (2017, September). Putting lifelong learning on the CEO agenda. *McKinsey Quarterly.* https://www.mckinsey.com/business-functions/people-and-organizational-performance/our-insights/putting-lifelong-learning-on-the-ceo-agenda

Etzkowitz, H., & Leydesdorff, L. (2000). The dynamics of innovation: From national systems and 'Mode 2' to a triple helix of university-industry-government relations. *Research Policy, 29,* 109–123.

Feldman, N. (2013). *Cool war: The United States, China and the future of global competition.* New York, NY: Random House.

Frank, D., & Gabler, J. (2006). *Reconstructing the university: Worldwide shifts in academia in the 20th century.* Stanford, CA: Stanford University Press.

Frey, C. B., & Osborne, M. A. (2013). *The future of employment: How susceptible are jobs to computerisation.* www.oxfordmartin.ox.ac.uk/downloads/academic/The_Future_of_Employment.pdf

Frey, C. B., & Osborne, M. A. (2015). *Technology at work: The future of innovation and employment.* www.oxfordmartin.ox.ac.uk/downloads/reports/Citi_GPS_Technology_Work.pdf

Galimberti, F. (2002). *Economics e pazzia. Crisi finanziarie di ieri e di oggi.* Bari, Italy: Laterza.

Gallino, L. (2011). *Finanzcapitalismo. La civiltà del denaro in crisi.* Torino, Italy: Einaudi.

Garin, E. (1996). La concezione dell'università in Italia nell'età del Rinascimento. In R. Greci (Ed.), *Il Pragmatismo Degli Intellettuali. Origini e Primi Sviluppi dell'Istituzione Universitaria.* Turin, Italy: Scriptorum (essay taken from Les Universités Européennes du XIVe au XVIIIe siècle: aspects et problèmes, Acts of the International Symposium for the 600th anniversary of the Jagiellonian University of Kraków, 6–8 May 1964).

Gherardini, A. (2015). *Squarci nell'avorio.* Firenze, Italy: Firenze University Press.

Governa, F. (2015). Città e processi di urbanizzazione, fra tendenze e modelli. *Scienze del Territorio, 3,* 68–77.

Grilli, E. (2005). *Crescita e sviluppo delle Nazioni. Teorie, strategie e risultati.* Milano, Italy: UTET Università.

Hansen, M. T., & Birkinshaw, J. (2006, June). The innovation value chain. *Harvard Business Review.*

Homer Haskins, C. (2013). *The rise of universities.* Ithaca, NY: Cornell University Press (Original work published 1923).

International Monetary Fund. (2019). *World Economic Outlook Database.* https://www.imf.org/en/Publications/WEO/weo-database/2019/October/download-entire-database

Kerr, C. (1995). *The use of universities.* Cambridge, MA: Harvard University Press.

Keynes, J. M. (1963). *Essays in persuasion.* New York, NY: W. W. Norton & Co.

Khanna, P. (2016). *Connectography. Mapping the future of global civilization.* New York, NY: Random House.

Kline Cohn, S. (2008). *Lust for liberty: The politics of social revolt in medieval Europe, 1200–1425.* Boston, MA: Harvard University Press.

Lacaita, C. G. (1973). *Istruzione e sviluppo industriale in Italia, 1859–1914*. Firenze, Italy: Giunti.

Latour, B. (2018). *Down to earth: Politics in the new climatic regime*. London: John Wiley & Sons.

Mann, C. C. (2011). *1493: Uncovering the new world Columbus created* (A. A. Knopf, Ed., Penguin). New York, NY: Random House.

Marzano, F. (2008). *Economia della crescita. Dalla teoria classica alle controversie fra contemporanei*. Milano, Italy: Mondadori Università.

McKinsey & Company. (2017, December). *Jobs lost, jobs gained: Workforce transitions in a time of automation*.

McNeill, J. R., & Engelke, P. (2014). *The great acceleration: An environmental history of the Anthropocene since 1945*. Cambridge, MA: The Belknap Press of Harvard University Press.

Milanovic, B. (2016, 5 July). This chart reveals the most dramatic change in incomes since the first industrial revolution. *World Economic Forum*. http://tinyurl.com/j62z266

Moretti, E. (2012). *The new geography of jobs*. Boston, MA: Houghton Mifflin Harcourt.

Morozov, E. (2016). *Silicon valley. I signori del silicio* (Italian ed.). Torino, Italy: Codice Edizioni.

Normann, R., & Ramirez, R. (1993). *From value chain to value constellation: Designing interactive strategy, business, medicine*. London: Wiley.

Piketty, T. (2013). *Le Capital au XXIe siècle*. Paris, France: Éditions du Seuil [English translation. (2014). *Capital in the twenty-first century*. Cambridge, MA: Harvard University Press].

Quinn, J. B. (1992). *Intelligent enterprise. A knowledge and service based paradigm for industry*. New York, NY: The Free Press.

R&D Magazine. (2019). *Global R&D funding forecast*, Annual Study. https://www.rdworldonline.com/2019-rd-global-funding-forecast/

Rifkin, J. (2000). *Age of access: The new culture of hypercapitalism*. London: Penguin.

Roco, M. C., Bainbridge W. S., Tonn B., & Whitesides G. (2013). *Convergence of knowledge, technology and society: Beyond convergence of nano-bio-info-cognitive technologies*. Berlin, Germany: Springer.

Rullani, E. (2004). *Economia della conoscenza. Creatività e valore nel capitalismo delle reti*. Roma, Italy: Carocci.

Sassen, S. (1991). *The global city: New York, London, Tokyo*. Princeton, NJ: Princeton University Press.

Secchi, B. (2013). *La città dei ricchi e la città dei poveri*. Roma-Bari, Italy: Laterza.

Solow, R. M. (2000). *Growth theory: An exposition*. New York, NY: Oxford Business Press.

Stiglitz, J. E. (2015). *The great divide: Unequal societies and what we can do about them*. New York, NY: Columbia Business School.

Stiglitz, J. E. (2018). *Invertire la rotta: disuguaglianza e crescita economica* (Italian ed.). Bari, Italy: Laterza.

Sugrue, T. J. (2014). *The origins of the urban crisis: Race and inequality in postwar Detroit*. Princeton, NJ: Princeton University Press.

Sundararajan, A. (2016). *The sharing economy. The end of employment and the rise of crowd-based capitalism*. Cambridge, MA: MIT Press.

The World Bank. (2019). *World Bank Open Data*. https://data.worldbank.org/

The World Bank. (2020). *DataBank*. databank.worldbank.org

Triventi, M. (2012). *Sistemi universitari comparati. Riforme, assetti istituzionali e accessibilità agli studenti*. Milano, Italy: Bruno Mondadori.

United Nations. (2019). *World population prospects 2019.* UN Department of Economic and Social Affairs. https://population.un.org/wpp/

Viesti, G. (2016). *Università in declino. Un Rapporto sugli atenei italiani da Nord a Sud.* Roma, Italy: Donzelli.

Wong, S. Y. (1991). The evolution of social science instruction, 1900–86: A cross-national study. *Sociology of Education, 64*(1), 33–47.

World Economic Forum. (2016, January). The future of jobs. Employment skills and workforce strategy for the fourth industrial revolution. *WEF.* http://hdl.voced.edu.au/10707/393272

2

EDUCATION, RESEARCH, ENTREPRENEURSHIP, SOCIETY

Comparing models

Faced by today's assortment of accelerating challenges, universities are taking an evermore central role in the advance of knowledge and the development of society, putting in place a series of actions that range from education and research to technological innovation and community outreach initiatives. The actual idea of what a university stands for in contemporary society, what are its tasks, privileges and resources, is far more complex than the traditional concept of the role held by this thousand-year-old institution.

Society's expectations about the role of universities are now quite different. Universities must without doubt produce cutting-edge research and sound education. They must also be major players in developing their local areas, creating and spreading innovation, and sharing, to the best of their ability, knowledge generated through research, and they may turn to channels other than scientific production in the strictest sense. They must also be able to influence the drafting of public policies.

More in general, as we have seen, even within conventional university business, universities have been in the grip of contradiction for some time, caught between more and more complex requests on the one side, and ever scarcer resources, on the other. This has induced many universities (public ones included) in Europe and elsewhere, to interact with a much bigger pool of stakeholders than in the past and this, in turn, means that they have to respond to a wider range of sometimes contradictory requests (Clark, 1998).

On the one hand, governments and a wide swathe of actors from the productive sector have started to see universities as primary players in the dynamics of local and regional development and innovation, like a sort of community development agency and a catalyst of resources and energies scattered across the territory (Etzkowitz et al., 2000). On the other hand, the growing trend for decentralized networks that produce and spread knowledge from all sides, flanked by the

DOI: 10.4324/9781003231004-03

34 Education, research, entrepreneurship, society

plummeting loss of faith in the technical and scientific expertise fielded by worthy institutions, is forcing universities to rebuild trust and credibility. Among other measures, they are placing themselves more explicitly at the service of society, producing good knowledge that is both accessible and democratic. At the same time, universities are up against a progressive cut in unitary resources (the amount that governments had been willing to spend on each student at the time of "universities for the elite" cannot be transferred to the model of "universities for the masses", let alone to the model of university education for all). Universities today are, therefore, trying to redefine their social usefulness by setting themselves new strategic objectives.

These tensions can naturally push in different and even opposite directions, but in general they are all heading towards greater accountability and the legitimization of tertiary education systems and individual universities, whosoever is promoting them.

Universities today, more than ever before, are not only responsible for forming human capital (traditionally their first mission) and producing knowledge (traditionally their second mission), but also for an assembly of things that are known collectively as their third mission. The burgeoning importance of the third mission is not an isolated process; rather it is tightly bound up in the changing role of universities in general, with echoes felt in teaching and research and naturally in the balances of governance.

For the most part, universities must all find their own way to have a positive impact on the planet's sustainable development and that of humankind. *Research* and *education* are certainly two of their most impactful undertakings (Figure 2.1). In research, for example, a responsible approach implies paying attention to the impact that all the phases of building and conducting a research project have on society, focusing particularly on the various actors involved, in line with the paradigm of Responsible Research and Innovation promoted by the European Commission.[6]

Other up-and-coming areas where the intention is to optimize social impact, especially in technical universities, are *technological transfer* and *entrepreneurial innovation*, as well as *outreach programmes* to interact with society. Entrepreneurial innovation means using technological innovation to create new tangible applications (and so new jobs), which can contribute towards tackling the great global challenges. Outreach programmes mean that universities must take a primary role in bringing scientific culture to the wider community through communication and information, as well as in defining public and private development policies.

The third and outer circle covers a wider range of actions that can have a positive impact on society, which can have more or less close connections with a university's main business and operations.

Starting from this general picture, we can look more closely at the emerging features and challenges in education, research and other areas, from scientific

6 https://ec.europa.eu/programmes/horizon2020/en/h2020-section/responsible-research-innovation.

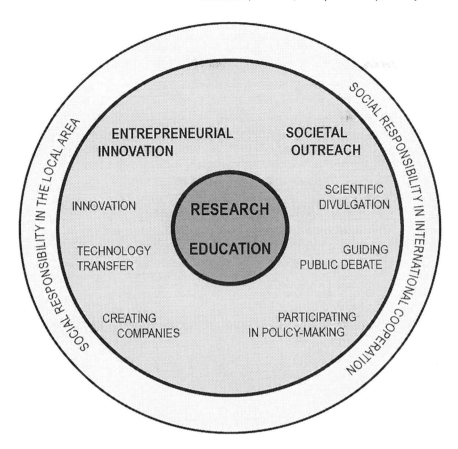

FIGURE 2.1   Actions relating to the social value of universities.

divulgation, steering public debate and influencing policies, to technological transfer, promoting innovation and contributing to local development. Our analysis will also extend to projects linked to social responsibility towards the local area or set up within a perspective of international cooperation.

In the next sections, our review will be positioned by levels, focusing separately on the national or international outlook, on the relationship between universities and stakeholders in particular areas, and on the initiatives put in place by individual universities. We will, therefore, discuss each of these areas in greater detail, starting with the evolution in education and the models by which it is guided, and then examining the transformations to research in an increasingly competitive global world, alongside the various implications of promoting technological innovation. Finally, we will explore how this innovation interacts with society and how it is spread.

36 Education, research, entrepreneurship, society

2.1 Education poised between disciplinarity and new pedagogical approaches

We are living in an increasingly intricate world where disciplines are becoming progressively more multifaceted and multi-layered. As a consequence, the various corpora of academic disciplines are becoming more complex, making it extremely difficult to find a balance between specialization and transversal skills.

A model that can address this twofold need is unlikely to consider transversal skills as "auxiliary", and so placed within specific targeted teaching, but rather as the outcome of a series of teaching methodologies where students are shown how to expand on these methods and develop them inductively. In other words, this model identifies knowledge and core skills (the basics of subject matter, methodology and tools), which are then taught to students (transferred) through courses and lessons on these topics, and soft skills, which are learnt (acquired) through special work methods and teaching models.

Today, outgoing students have often assembled a profile featuring a rich and complex set of competencies, they have experienced many different teaching approaches and their individual study pathways are more diversified than in the past, within and without the university system. These elements together point to the need of revisiting the different levels of education and the way profiles are structured, in order to reconcile the following needs:

- Demand from the job world, often inclined towards people with known and immediately employable competencies.
- The need to give students tools they can use in professional settings that are in constant change, by reconfiguring skills and adapting them to the context.
- The need to ensure that a selection of students will be taught advanced subject matter in their field, enabling them to pursue an active role in exploratory and cutting-edge research.
- The need to provide multi-disciplinary cross-functional skills.

At the same time, many scholars have noticed a change in the students' cognitive pathways, which has been gaining pace since the early part of this millennium as the result of widespread access to network technology and digital tools (Montedoro et al., 2020). Some studies have highlighted that technology requires interaction to be much faster than in the past. On the one hand, people become more adept at splitting their attention and multitasking while, on the other, their attention span is shorter and their cognitive ability lessened, especially their capacity for concentration, deep thought and reflection (Kahneman, 2011).

This development calls for teaching practices to be completed upturned, and more attention given to the efficacy of the learning process. Technical universities represent contexts that are naturally more exposed to the effects of change and must be the first to respond with suitable strategies.

2.1.1 Education in technical universities

Technical universities have played an important role in training professionals at the service of technological progress in society, first with the industrial transformation and now with the ongoing digital transformation. The educational models adopted in these contexts are traditionally and naturally preoccupied with shaping people who can be rapidly inserted into production and innovation processes. The generally remarkably close contact between universities and stakeholders from the industrial world has enabled education and training to evolve in line with the needs of the world of work, while, in parallel, research carried out in these universities was being used as an engine of innovation and transformation.

The specific features of the various countries and social and economic landscapes have, however, produced fairly different models. In Italy, the local context has been adopting the model of highly specialized technical universities that concentrate on engineering, architecture and design as the expression of studies geared towards technology and applied sciences. In other countries, technical tertiary education has been interpreted in a wider sense, to include basic and applied sciences. This diversity can be observed in Figure 2.2 where the average size of undergraduate programmes (average number of incoming students per year) is depicted versus the percentage of students enrolled in architecture, design or engineering, for some universities of reference. Figure 2.3 shows a similar picture for master's programmes. In many universities across Europe, the model of a technical university open to basic sciences was introduced over time, by gradually enlarging the range of subjects on offer or, sometimes, through agreements with other universities.

The social importance of technical education has increased alongside technological progress and the importance of technology in a country's economy, meaning that technical universities are taking a greater strategic lead within university systems in different countries and geographical regions. As a result, some of these universities have joined the magic circle of the most prestigious and internationally renowned institutes, becoming the place of choice for cutting-edge research and innovation. To this aim, some universities took the decision to concentrate on the upper echelons only, masters' and doctorates, paying less attention to undergraduate level, with major differences from country to country, and from university to university (see Figure 2.4).

Diversification between the undergraduate and postgraduate offer corresponds to their different functions and in some countries has become the established format, where the first level is seen as an essential tool to educate the workforce for the industrial world, and the higher levels as the forge turning out people who can create innovation and advanced research. This is particularly the case for universities in the English-speaking world and the Far East, but less so in mainland Europe, including Italy. In terms of the number of graduate programmes compared to undergraduate courses, research universities clearly have a much richer offer, while those in the traditional mould are inclined towards continuity from undergraduate to graduate level.

38 Education, research, entrepreneurship, society

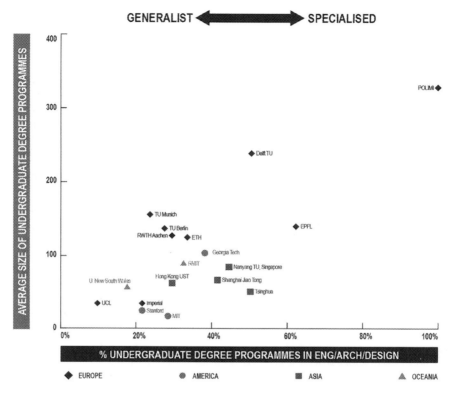

FIGURE 2.2 Average size of undergraduate degree programmes (*y*-axis) versus the percentages of undergraduate degree programmes focusing on engineering, architecture and design (*x*-axis) for a set of representative universities.

The differences in educational provision between various systems, countries or single universities do not stop here. Many other factors come into play, including per-student funding, the professor-student ratio, the average number of PhD students per faculty, and many other elements.

It is however clear that there is a tendency for strategies to be reasonably homogeneous within the world's great geographical blocks, where the best technical universities are the first to be called upon to drive the evolution of different teaching models ready to address the imposing challenges of innovation and sustainability.

2.1.2 Evolution of education models and ongoing changes

Education in the technical and scientific field tends to be, for obvious reasons, of an applied kind. The need to transfer the ability to think by projects and the training to produce innovation in the real world, as efficiently as possible, has led academics to question current education models for years. Among the most relevant issues faced in this context, we can mention: i) the need of creating differentiated

Education, research, entrepreneurship, society   **39**

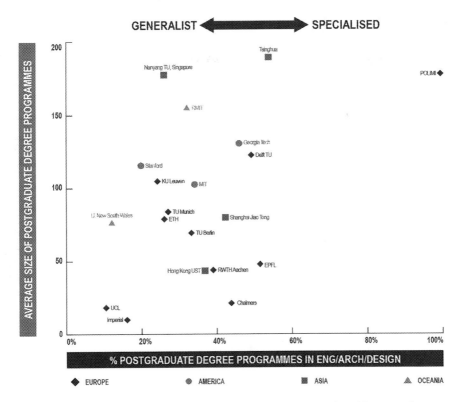

FIGURE 2.3   Average size of postgraduate degree programmes (*y*-axis) versus the percentages of master's degree programmes focusing on engineering, architecture and design (*x*-axis) for a set of representative universities.

and personalized teaching pathways whereby students can reach their potential, ii) the interconnection between the body of theory for each subject and its practical application, as well as the role of learning by projects, and the extension of this project-based approach in a more general perspective, iii) the way in which students have to be exposed to different multi-disciplinary situations, and the way in which interdisciplinary cross-fertilization steps can be introduced in the education process, and iv) the role of the evaluation step in the learning process. All these topics have to be examined more closely, to highlight some of the ongoing trends.

Personalization and differentiation in study paths

The students' motivation plays a central role in effective education and learning, as their capacity to play an active role in the training process. This objective is often pursued in teaching processes by actively involving students and using multimedia and interactive teaching methods. One element that spurs motivation, but which is

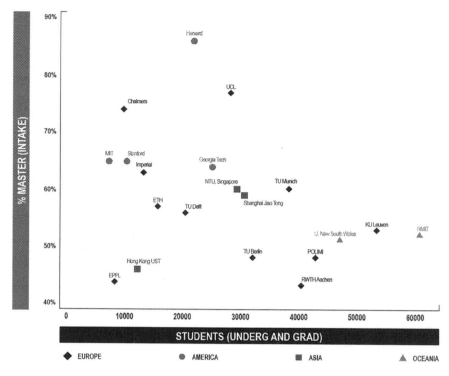

FIGURE 2.4 Incoming master's students as a percentage of all incoming students (undergraduates + master's students) in a reference group of universities.

somewhat overlooked, is being able to personalize the students' study programmes and so develop their individual interests and inclinations. The model adopted following the Bologna process has introduced severe limitations to the possibilities of personalization and programme customization, confining students to a particularly passive role within their own study paths.

Several possible directions emerge from observing models offering greater personalization that are also able to evade any opportunistic behaviour on the part of students (taking the easiest options). On the one side, the mentorship model is an essential element in the professors' set of tasks, to guide the choices of small groups of students and aid the definition of their study programmes, even considering courses selected outside the single university. On the other is the "meritocratic autonomy" model, which means rewarding students with greater freedom of choice proportionally to their results. The final model is to tap into networks of strategic partnerships and build personalized learning pathways, with students having access to a range of educational offers within a network of complementary universities.

Organizational models in teaching must be redesigned if the chosen route is to personalize learning paths in a flexible way within a wider educational provision, to be determined on the basis of personal interests, on the one side, and

Education, research, entrepreneurship, society **41**

the profiles and skills demanded by the job market, on the other. In addition, universities must take on the responsibility of acting as a continuous and trustworthy guide to help every student design a path most in line with their abilities and ambition, and which can match up to the openings on the job market and their role in society.

Relationship between theory and practice

The relationship between theory and practice is a topic of thought that runs throughout the evolution of pedagogic theory, with changes in emphasis along the way. In particular, the relationship between theoretical knowledge and the capacity to integrate and apply this knowledge to solve real problems in professional settings are central elements in technical and scientific education. Two basic aspects are affected, namely, the nature and breakdown of content within each lesson, and the classification of teaching into different levels, in part to follow the Bologna process rules (the 3 + 2 year model).

Regarding the first aspect, in the constructivist pedagogy debate, there is increasing emphasis on inductive forms of learning and on teaching methods slanted towards practice and practical application aspects. Having said this, recent scientific studies into the efficiency of learning processes based upon empirical evidence show that inductive and participatory teaching models are not necessarily the most efficacious.[7] Data show high efficacy only when joined by previous knowledge and experience, in other words, when students already know some essential concepts. Vice-versa, these models are proven to be highly efficacious, but only for a tiny percentage of students. Any teaching model must provide a good balance between face-to-face teaching and other learning models, whether by projects or participatory. What is instead fundamental is to involve the students thoroughly by asking for regular feedback and by transferring knowledge in units small enough not to induce cognitive overload.

With regard to the second aspect, in the traditional approach to technical-scientific training, the basics are taught early on, followed later by the technical and subject-specific theories and methodologies, starting first with sound advanced models and theories and then going on to the applications. This scheme describes a linear learning path that works best for people who already have the capability to think abstractly and typically generates high-level but standardized profiles.

Splitting university education into levels (considering the 3 + 2 setting of the Bologna process) totally upset this traditional model, with an increasing number of students who do not follow a linear trajectory but build their studies between the various levels according to a more liberal plan. This is probably the strongest empirical evidence to date in the change of cognitive models, which no longer trace individual training as a continuous line where the parts follow each other

---

7 visiblelearning@corwin.com, www.evidencebasedteaching.org.au/john-hattie-visible-learning/ – www.visiblelearning.com/content/visible-learning-research.

42 Education, research, entrepreneurship, society

sequentially. Instead, the end result is reached starting from an initial framework onto which new concepts and methods are added in successive stages.

This context brings up two primary trajectories. The first is to break down the material into smaller units, defined, as far as possible, by their theoretical content and practical, applicative and self-assessment elements, which can be slotted into different training cycles but not necessarily in a linear order. The second trajectory involves a general review of sequentiality and temporality in theoretical and applicative material, endorsing the possibility of students proceeding through their studies in a non-linear way.

Learning by projects

The laboratory training paradigm, as a project-based inductive teaching model, enables the transfer of methodological and adaptive capacities in conjunction with multi-disciplinary skills. Work that is focused on solving project-based problems consolidates knowledge in the subject because methods and instrumental skills are applied practically. At the same time, this approach develops the students' capacity to reconfigure knowledge in function of the context, and so help them reorganize their cognitive and learning ability.

This paradigm must necessarily include increasing levels of complexity, both in how the problems are set and in how the solutions are delineated. It must, in other words, progressively embrace an experimental model where tackling increasing difficulties and learning from one's errors become an integral part of the teaching process.

Students learn from these experiences how to develop their organizational skills inductively, and how to plan and manage projects, as well as self-organization and entrepreneurship, which are necessary to handle the ongoing changes to professional roles. Working by projects is a particularly good way for transferring relational skills within teams, although participation models are not necessarily the best way for people to achieve subject-specific and disciplinary knowledge (Bonaiuti et al., 2017).

Considerations about teaching models moving in the direction of progressive and experimental education are often coupled with debates on the spaces that suit learning best, whether physical or virtual. This topic is particularly important as technology is evolving fast, especially for technical and scientific universities, where learning by projects is a well-consolidated method.

The current stage is defined by a culture of progressive and experimental education that extends beyond universities, as highlighted by the growing number of FabLab networks, makerspaces and incubators. With this in mind, technical and scientific university education should be the next testing ground for new experimental models that can apply the most advanced paradigms of digitalization and connectivity. Backed by the growing worldwide wealth of experimental and instrumental knowledge, the challenge now appears to be integrating and building up available resources and areas within a "cyber-physical" teaching environment.

Education, research, entrepreneurship, society **43**

These are integrated spaces and experimental units where students from different backgrounds and universities can become familiar with technologies, learning how to use them and how to adapt them to various needs and situations, experimenting with a combination of analogical and digital techniques, manual skills and advanced technology.

Multi-disciplinary work

We understand multi-disciplinarity to be primarily the possibility of learning how to dialogue and understand languages outside those of a specific subject, combined with the opportunity of applying one's skills to complex issues and situations that need the input of many people and functions. The ensuing interaction can place students in the position of having to understand cognitive models that differ from their own, and so transfer their own capacity to conceptualize problems to this situation, embracing new points of view.

Furthermore, collaborative work in multi-disciplinary environments can be the occasion for people to acquire a set of different specializations, gain familiarity with other technical and technological spheres and, through various projects inductively develop new skills outside their own initial arena (Cuseo, 1997).

An open mindset can blossom and thrive in a multi-disciplinary environment, alongside a type of holistic overview of problems; if the space is there, together they can beget new professional roles outside the subjects per se. They are, therefore, a favourable environment for true transdisciplinary experimentation, which occupies the niches "between the subjects", intercepting emerging problem areas.

Within this perspective, there can be apparently opposing training needs that address vastly different objectives. We can list at least three.

The first is linked to training people so they are ready for specific professions. The requirement to educate professional classes is deeply enrooted in the technical universities' model, but it too is evolving rapidly with the demand to place know-how alongside disciplinary skills within the new professional settings. Multi-disciplinary skills in similar settings can be engendered through training processes where a sound specialist grounding is joined by the ability to understand the models and languages of other subject sets. In this case as well, there are many possible hybrid forms, and they must be guided with a view to personalizing the learning process.

The second objective is linked to education for the frontiers of scientific and technological research. Within the framework of increasingly independent bachelor's and master's programmes, which dip into different student pools, it now seems inevitable that this need will be satisfied through greater integration between master's and doctorate studies. One method could be to place master's students in differentiated tracks and then steer selected groups in the direction of more advanced material from the start of their course.

The third objective is true interdisciplinary education. By personalizing the studies of students sufficiently able academically and eclectic in their interests, this approach can act as an incubator in new discipline areas, taking the selected ones

44 Education, research, entrepreneurship, society

along hitherto unexplored paths. In this case, even more than in the previous two, the professor's responsibility and role in guiding the students is crucial to ensure, at least, a high level of quality and tight control against the risk of unsuccess.

In designing an education programme, we must not overlook all those initiatives that provide cultural enrichment and expand a student's skillset during their university life, including their activity outside the formal curricula. When we define university education as a life experience, we are also referring to the physical places that students visit, their social relationships, all the occasions for complementary learning that take place outside official timetables and programme schedules that help to create rich personalities.

This element of education can actually define a university and be its unique selling point alongside its curricular quality, thereby joining the set of factors that make up its attractiveness and reputation (Graham, 2018).

Continuous and self-evaluation

The current model of evaluation is still based closely on the concept of final exams, but it is no longer sufficient to ensure an efficacious process of learning. In many studies, it has been found that, if the evaluation process is repeated several times on smaller teaching units, it lightens the students' cognitive load, and is more attuned with the cognitive processes of current generations. This, however, must not result in a parcelling up of topics to the detriment of overall preparation in the subject (Calvani, 2009), therefore, there must always be tests to verify the student's comprehensive mastery of any given discipline.

It is also important to combine different evaluation methods, and, alongside the more mechanical and systematic checking of knowledge, the procedure can include dialogue and critical debate, the development of analytical elaborations and conceptual syntheses, and project assessment.

A second important element to quantify learning is to introduce student self-assessment and peer to peer assessment methods. These techniques have the added benefit that students will "own" their results, while also improving their critical and evaluations skills.

2.2 Scientific research poised between impact and exploring new frontiers

The facet of research entered universities roughly midway through the 19th century, running alongside their original mission of teaching and educating. This phase is often defined as the Academic Revolution (Jencks et al., 1968), and was the first step in a sweeping transformation to the university model, so that, over the past century, academic education and research leadership gradually pivoted from the European to the North American system.

Initially, this process was played out in a setting firmly committed to driving research and innovation in the technical and scientific field, that had helped to fuel

Education, research, entrepreneurship, society **45**

the Second Industrial Revolution. During this first stage, existing universities were redefining their mission, an undertaking bolstered by universities of a new type entering the scene, among which the Massachusetts Institute of Technology (MIT) and Stanford University in the United States, and Europe's technological universities. The new universities were the outcome of a determined focus on technical and scientific subjects and the resolute drive of local production and manufacturing systems, which often backed them financially with the intention of making them the engine of development, obviously through advanced training but also through technological transfer. During this process, doctorate programmes were put on a formal footing, evolving from the mediaeval "licence" to teach in an academic setting to preparing students for a career in research. While Germany provided the model for this transformation, thoroughly overhauling its education system in the early 1800s, the United States hastened the change and, from the mid-19th century, all major universities introduced doctorate programmes.

In the mid-20th century, academic research was given another prod, with new economic theories that saw technological progress as the gateway to national economic growth.[8] These new visions helped to raise the importance of research institutes and the scale of the resources they received. By the late 1980s, they were being seen as the main motor of development within what we know as the "knowledge economy" (Quinn, 1992; Drucker, 2011).[9] In traditional economies, natural resources, work and capital have always been the main elements of competition and wealth, but in modern economies the creation, transfer, diffusion and use of knowledge are basic ingredients in the development of social well-being.

The American Super Research University (SRU) model took hold in these decades, soon becoming an international exemplar and often seen as the key for explaining the gap in technological innovation that was gradually leaving the European system behind (Freeman et al., 2004). An important factor in this process was the growing public backing of the function played by these institutions, along with the socialization of the idea that they performed an essential collective benefit in retaining the world's economic leadership in North America (Baker, 2008; Baker, 2018). By the end of the 20th century, in just a few decades, the cost of research in these universities had hit levels impossible to match in Europe, undergirded by conspicuous public and private funding. Overly complex and costly administrative apparatus started leveraging on the SRUs' growing international reputation to operate on a global scale, entering into competition with all the other university systems in both teaching and research. Global attractiveness quickly became a distinctive factor in this model. With their commanding autonomy, SRUs could select their researchers from among the world's greatest talents, based on factors like productivity, impact and ability to attract funds in a formidably competitive landscape.

---

8 The neoclassical theory first and the endogenous growth models later started to emphasize the role that human capital, innovation and other intangible factors can play in generating economic development and the growth of productivity (Solow, 2000; Grilli, 2005; Marzano, 2008).

9 *Towards knowledge societies*: UNESCO world reports, 2005.

At the onset of the new millennium, the SRUs evolved once more, strengthening their bonds with the corporate world, their local ecosystems and the networks of global knowledge open to them. Several particularly successful models, Silicon Valley in California and the Boston – New York axis, *in primis*, originated spontaneously because of particular features in the local ecosystem linked to the university. For example, the high number of students completing a doctorate, well beyond the local requirements, produced a surplus of PhD holders who recast themselves and set up their own highly innovative companies. These successful models were the trigger for the "Second Academic Revolution", which shifted the emphasis to research that could produce short-term measurable impacts on the economic and production systems, and coax a continuing process of technological transfer and new entrepreneurship (Etzkowitz, 2003). The outcome was the "university-company" cooperation model, where funding for research is directed, more or less subtly, towards fields with a high impact on productivity and good technological transfer returns. This model also embodies true entrepreneurial strategies, introducing within universities functions that are not strictly proper to education and research, such as finance and real estate.

The chart in Figure 2.5 clearly highlights several models of reference, giving the spending per student in absolute terms and as a percentage (public funding,

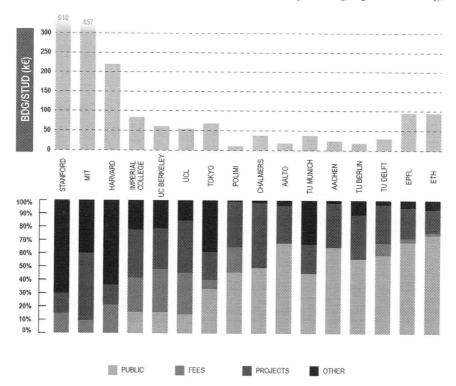

FIGURE 2.5 Spending per student and percentage of funding sources in several universities of reference.

Source: Financial statements published by universities for 2017

Education, research, entrepreneurship, society **47**

student fees, projects and other sources of finance). The first thing to note is that the management model in several private schools of excellence is like those of "real" companies their budgets are in an order of magnitude higher than those of other universities and are sourced from operations not directly linked to education or research (financial or real estate business). It is also clear that the model relating to top American schools is different from that used in many European universities, with their lower financing (apart from Switzerland's two technical universities) and general public status.

And so, over the past two decades, within today's very uniform university arrangements exposed as they are to the dynamics of globalization, SRUs have become the model of reference that guides the reform policies in many international university systems, especially in Europe and Asia. University actors are being pressured into taking an active role in powering innovation and entrepreneurship in their local regions. The principles underpinning these transformations are based on driving up the attractiveness of universities for prominent and distinguished professors and researchers, and on measuring the productivity and impact of academic initiatives, with the aim, in part, of further concentrating resources, especially public resources, in universities where research is high on the agenda.

However, if top-down policies are used to encourage a model that emerged spontaneously in North America, the outcomes may not be fully foreseen or foreseeable; the trajectories of evolution may be very diverse, especially in systems with different economic and development cycles. In Asia, for instance, the economy is in expansion and the growing resources are directed towards selected institutes; additionally, the universities themselves face fewer restrictions and change is happening at a faster pace. As a result, the academic body is steered towards responding more efficiently and rapidly to the needs of scientific production where impact can be measured, and which can easily intercept the more highly visible topics. So Asian universities are climbing the international rankings in record time.

In Europe, the economic cycle is stagnant or in recession, public funding is progressively wilting and new sources of financing must be sought; the policies to reform university systems produce totally different effects and the SRU model seems rather out of reach. The chart in Figure 2.5 shows very clearly that the American SRU model differs substantially from that used in many European universities, with their decidedly lower financing (apart from Switzerland's two technical universities) and their predominantly public status.

In the light of this evolving landscape, an analytical comparison between the many university systems on the international stage can provide scope for reflection on the impact of policies introduced as part of various reforms, and on the strategies that could play out in the future.

2.2.1 Scientific productivity

In today's challenging global competitive arena, scientific productivity is an interesting factor to analyse and for making comparisons between university models,

48 Education, research, entrepreneurship, society

although the criticism is that it gives a partial and distorted picture. Evaluating research on the basis of bibliometric indicators is of little use in the many disciplines that do not wrap up research with a publication. Even in the bibliometric sectors, the exclusive use of quantitative indicators has been criticized, as they only cover aspects like number of publications, number of citations and "h-index" - like impact metrics.

Despite all these quandaries, productivity and impact indicators for scientific production are strategic because they have a bearing on competitivity among universities vying for public resources and positions in international rankings. The *QS World University Rankings* includes the number of citations and h-index in the set of indicators it uses to determine the position of a university (the two indicators together account for 20% in classifications relating to architecture and 30% in those relating to engineering). In the same way, the *Times Higher Education Ranking* gives a 30% weighting to scientific citations.

The analysis of the past 20 years' worth of bibliometric results highlights a few interesting points that occur on an international scale, first and foremost the substantial and constantly increasing number of scientific papers produced every year (Figure 2.6). The growing trend for productivity comes with its own set of features, linked to the researchers' area of provenance and the subject field where the published works slot in. If we look at the total number of works produced (Figure 2.6a), European universities top the list and have been outdistancing the North Americans evermore markedly since the early 2000s. The same graph shows that the highest percentage increase in productivity is in the Far East, where universities have nearly bridged the gap to their North American counterparts in the span of 20 years or so (Figure 2.6a).

The dynamics of productivity change when we consider scientific output in different areas (see Figures 2.6b, c and d). In natural sciences and engineering, above all, university productivity in the East is threatening Europe's hegemony, and North America was left behind ages ago (Figure 2.6c). The picture changes when we look at life sciences and medicine, where European and North American universities are still jousting for the top spot, travelling at similar rates of growth in productivity and keeping well ahead of their colleagues in the Far East. Factors such as an ageing population can probably come into play in this area.

Similar considerations can be made by concentrating on scientific production in universities for more recent years (Figures 2.7 and 2.8). Here, also, the general trend indicates an increase in the number of scientific products, with higher-than-average performance in the two Chinese universities included in our study (Tsinghua and Shanghai Jiao Tong). It is also clear that some universities remain more focused on their vocation than others. For example, from a comparison between the two, it is clear that MIT's research strategy is less closely focused than that of Georgia Tech. MIP's productivity is generally higher than Georgia Tech's (Figures 2.7 and 2.8), but this difference is lower when looking at Engineering and Technology publications only (Figure 2.6b).

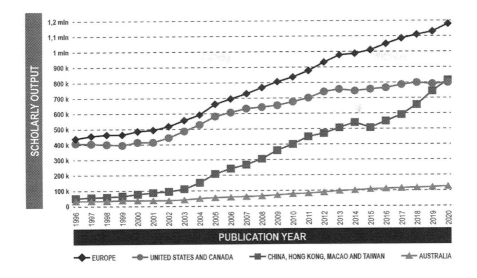

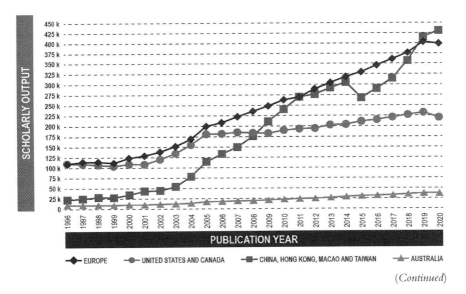

(Continued)

FIGURE 2.6 (Continued)

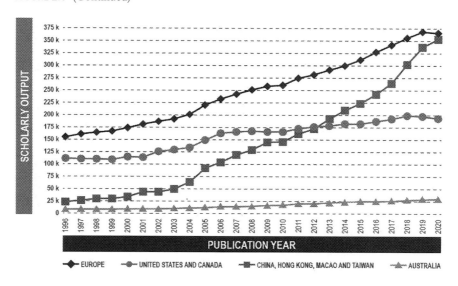

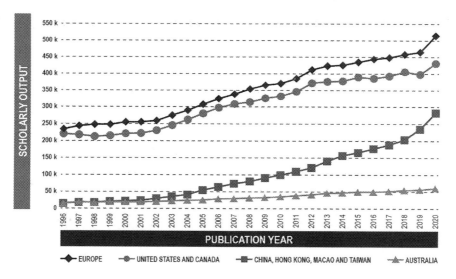

FIGURE 2.6 Scientific productivity (number of products) in (a) all areas, (b) engineering and technology, (c) natural sciences and (d) life sciences and medicine in Europe, North America, Far East and Australia.

Source: Scopus – SciVal, QS classification areas

Education, research, entrepreneurship, society 51

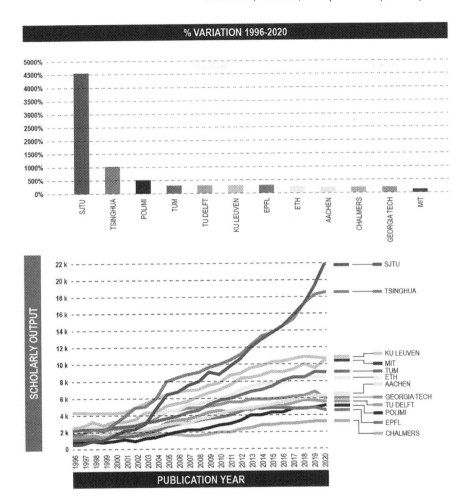

FIGURE 2.7 Scientific productivity (number of products) and percentage variation in productivity for some universities of reference.

Source: Scopus – publications in all areas

2.2.2 Research topics balancing focus and prominence

In order to analyse research by *topics* of interest for the researchers, we can direct our analysis to the second level of interest, keeping in mind that the limits discussed for biometrical analyses still apply here.

52 Education, research, entrepreneurship, society

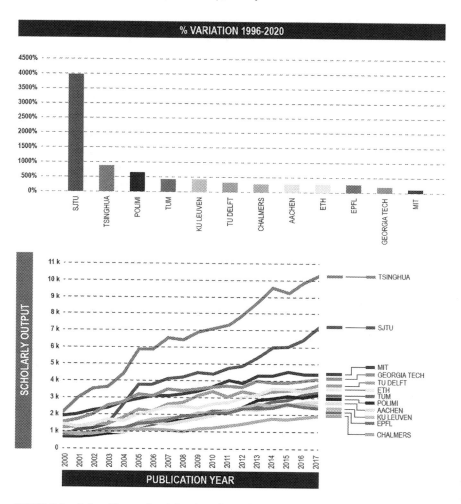

FIGURE 2.8 Scientific productivity (number of products) and percentage variation in productivity for some universities of reference.

Source: Scopus – publications in engineering and technology

Starting from a classification of the *topics* where scientific production mostly concentrates, *prominence* value can be associated with every topic,[10,11,12] where the "prominence" is an indicator defined by Scopus-SciVal to compute the *momentum* gained by a specific research topic in recent years.

10 Prominence is based upon a number of citations, visualizations and citation scores – equivalent to impact.
11 www.elsevier.com/solutions/scival/releases/topic-prominence-in-science.
12 Only the most prominent topics at global level were used in the chart (top 1% – i.e. only the first 1,000 topics of prominence out of 96,000 publication topics listed by Scopus).

Education, research, entrepreneurship, society   **53**

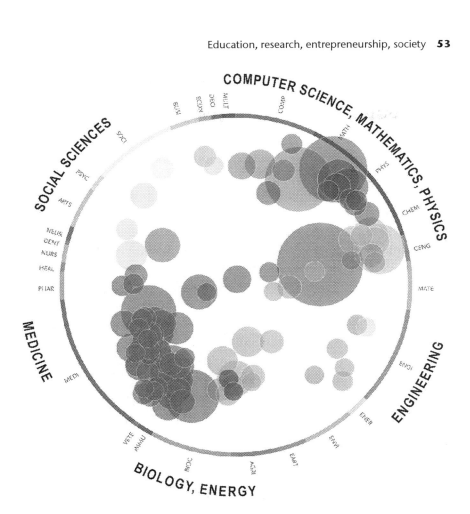

FIGURE 2.9   Prominence.

A graphic map for the most *prominent* topics can be thus created to gain an *identity card* for research topics of greatest *impact* in the period of reference. Figure 2.9 is an example of a *prominence* map, where every bubble in the chart represents a research topic, the size of the bubble indicates the number of publications on that topic in the period of reference, and the bubble's position is linked to the area where it belongs (computer science, chemistry, mathematics and physics, engineering, energy and biology, medicine and social sciences).

The *prominence* maps in Figure 2.10 highlight different focus models in nine universities. From top to bottom, every line gives three examples of universities with a similar level of focus on high prominence topics. The top line shows the prominence map for three technical universities that concentrate on engineering, computer science, physics and chemistry (Politecnico di Milano, Chalmers and TU Delft). The middle row gives three technical universities that instead concentrate most on research topics that are not strictly limited to engineering, but are also

54 Education, research, entrepreneurship, society

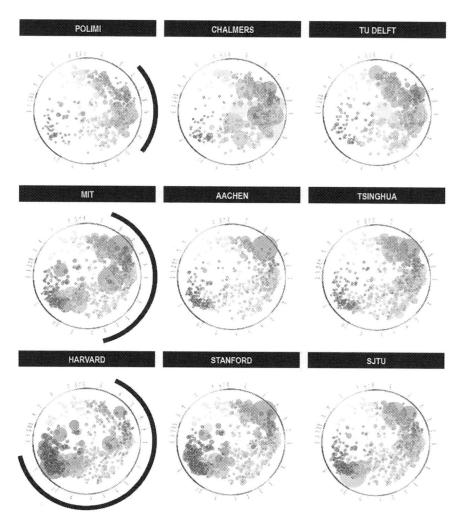

FIGURE 2.10 Prominence maps for several universities.
Source: Scopus, SciVal (2013–2017)

open towards energy, biology, genetics and medicine (MIT, Aachen and Tsinghua). The bottom line gives three universities with a wide range of topics of interest, with a prominent place given to biology and medicine (Harvard, Stanford and Shanghai Jiao Tong).

Looking at the *prominence* maps, we can see that the general trend for technical universities is to broaden their sphere of interest and turn their eye to topics in the field of life sciences and medicine. This trend has probably been encouraged by global challenges that direct funding policies.

2.2.3 Education and the place of doctorate studies

The increasing value that knowledge is acquiring in many economies and societies, mostly in the western world, is radically changing the professional experts capable of upholding the processes of creating, improving and sharing new knowledge. The place and purpose of a research doctorate are, therefore, changing continuously and fundamentally. There are now many more research doctors than 15 years ago, with the United States, Germany, the United Kingdom and India heading the list of countries turning out the greatest number (Figures 2.11 and 2.12). In the fields we are examining, about 40% of all new PhD holders in the OECD area are in science, technology, engineering and mathematics (STEM subjects), and this percentage goes up to 58% if we also include subjects in the medical and health field.

A more accurate analysis of the ratio of PhD students to permanent teaching staff presents a very convoluted picture, shown in Figure 2.13. Swiss universities (ETH and EPFL) hold the record with six to eight PhD students per professor, against a relatively low overall number of 10,000 to 20,000 students (shown on the

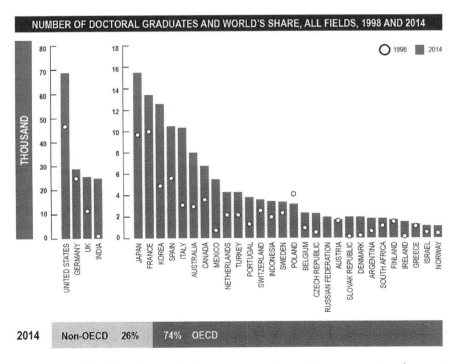

FIGURE 2.11 Number of research doctors in several countries: a comparison between 1998 and 2014.[13]

---

13 OECD Science, Technology and Innovation Outlook 2016 – DOI:https://dx.doi.org/10.1787/sti_in_outlook-2016-en.

56 Education, research, entrepreneurship, society

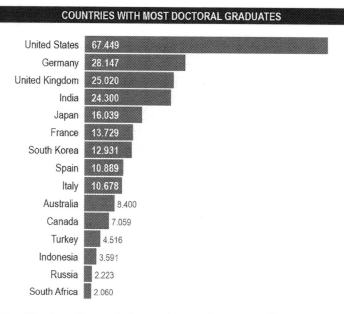

FIGURE 2.12 Number of research doctors in several countries.[14]

x-axis). Aachen University's PhD student-to-professor ratio is similar but within the much larger student population typical of a public European university (about 45,000 students).

The ratio is between 3 and 4 in most universities in our analysis (Delft, Stanford, MIT, TU Berlin, TU Munich, Shanghai Jiao Tong and Tsinghua), while a few European universities hover at about one PhD student per professor (CentraleSupélec, Politecnico di Milano and KU Leuven).

For now, we are still wondering what the right number of PhD students should be globally (Cyranoski et al., 2011), but it is obvious that a research doctorate should be reinterpreted as an opportunity to give postgraduates training in a range of different professions expected to play a leading part in creating, managing and sharing research and innovation, whether academic or not.

2.3 University entrepreneurship within emerging innovation paradigms

As we have seen, the Second Industrial Revolution went hand in hand with the Academic Revolution. This process, in turn, led to academic institutions widening their mission and a new kind of university took centre stage, one not given over to

---

14 OECD Science, Technology and Innovation Outlook 2016 – DOI:https://dx.doi.org/10.1787/sti_in_outlook-2016-en.

Education, research, entrepreneurship, society 57

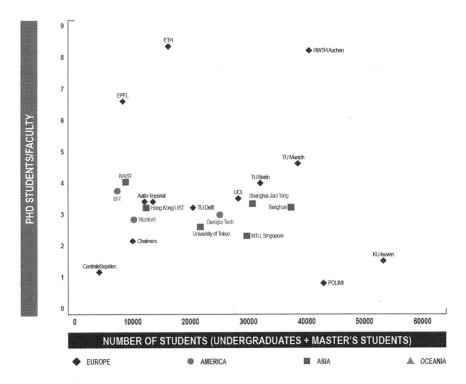

FIGURE 2.13 Number of research doctors per faculty vs number of undergraduate and master's students.[15]

education alone but also pledged to research, especially in the technical and scientific field, and thus able to accelerate the rate at which entire countries could "do" innovation. The Third and especially the Fourth Industrial Revolution provided the bases for universities to wield more influence and expand their sphere of action. This "Second Academic Revolution" built up to the invention of "entrepreneurial universities" (Etzkowitz, 2003). Within this model, universities are expected to play a more prominent role in industrial and production ecosystems, and thereby assist the economies of innovation by encouraging collaborations with the private sector and by promoting new forms of entrepreneurship among their own research groups and academic subjects.[16]

In line with this trend, the development of new technological applications or investing in start-ups and spin-offs is increasingly seen as an integral part of the academic mission. In particular, in settings where challenges play out at the borders of

---

15 OECD Science, Technology and Innovation Outlook 2016 – DOI:https://dx.doi.org/10.1787/sti_in_outlook-2016-en.
16 Farnam Jahanian, Carnegie Mellon University, World Economic Forum, 2018.

58 Education, research, entrepreneurship, society

several subjects, promoting entrepreneurship is regarded as an extremely powerful way for universities to act as economic and social development accelerators. At the same time, as universities are developing their own entrepreneurial side, local systems and companies that embody a prevalence of SMEs and a focus on mature and highly competitive sectors are finding it increasingly difficult to fuel new processes of innovation, and will often be excluded from the new dynamics of producing and circulating knowledge.

To understand these dynamics and the potential role that universities, especially the ones with a technical and scientific focus, can play in promoting innovation and entrepreneurship, we must first look at the two facets of transformation that defined the beginnings of the 21st century. The first is the radical change at the core of technological innovation and the new paradigms of innovation that transformed the processes through which knowledge is shared, transferred and applied. The second is connected to the first and consists of the new relationships universities create within their ecosystems.

2.3.1 Technological evolution and innovation paradigms

The Fourth Industrial Revolution is often associated with the technological model of connectivity and integration between the physical and virtual worlds, achieved through the pervasiveness of digital networks. This aspect has certainly acted as a highly influential lever for change in the transformations of the past 20 years, but other factors related to the nature of recent technological evolution and consequent innovation paradigms could determine long-term changes, with potentially radical and unexpected impacts in the near future. The main two factors are:

- The ongoing convergence between different research and innovation domains, especially in the sphere of artificial sciences (e.g. intelligent algorithms, nanotechnology, materials, processes, systems) and natural sciences (e.g. biological and medical sciences). The integration between ICT and neurosciences is particularly pervasive, with new technologies exploiting the soaring potential of diffused elaboration to replicate highly complex cognitive processes, which can then be utilized in many different fields of application (Mitchell, 2019).
- The transformation of innovation dynamics themselves, which have been broadened from the confined boundaries of R&D companies' departments and canters, to become open processes (Hansen et al., 2006). New paradigms have been emerging where networks of actors are collectively contributing to innovation advancements, linking established companies, start-ups, universities and even civil society.

The first factor referring to the convergence between technological and applicative domains closes the gap between "sciences of the artificial" and "natural sciences", opening into landscapes where the boundaries of organic and inorganic sciences are blurred. This process starts with the integration between ICT and

Education, research, entrepreneurship, society **59**

neurosciences, which already began midway through the last century with cybernetical studies and the first computer simulations of neural networks (Amari, 1977; Hopfield, 1982; Amit, 1989). It has now reached a greater level of technological maturity, helped by the evolving data processing power of computers, diffused connectivity, miniaturized sensors and the new robotics frontiers (Khushf, 2007; Kline, 2015). This change marks a revolutionary paradigmatic shift: for the first time in human history, machines are not only able to process data quicker and in higher quantity than humans but are now able to replicate complex learning processes and mirror elaborate human functions, such as solving new problems, decision-making, language cognition and, in some cases, artistic creativity. Additionally, in more radical applications and simulation, where impacts can be somewhat opaque, cognitive technologies can be integrated with biological systems to produce hybrid organisms capable of even higher performances (Kurtweil, 2013; Harari, 2017).

Since the start of the new millennium, this convergence process has been eyed with increasing interest and has become a special context of reference for steering policies of research and innovation. Among the various initiatives that accelerate this dynamic, the report "Converging technologies for improving human performance: Nanotechnology, biotechnology, information technology and cognitive science (NBIC)", promoted by the American National Science Foundation in 2002, has had an impact that has been going beyond the US borders, influencing numerous research policies both in Europe and in Asia. This highly progressive vision brings with it controversial perspectives, numerous ethical questions and a growing need to develop models of critical interpretation and impact prediction (Grebenshchikova, 2016). In particular, a different vision emerges in Europe, which balances the strongly technocratic approach of the United States and assigns a critical and guiding role to social sciences and humanities in the ongoing convergence process (Loverige, 2008; De Martin, 2016).

The trend described earlier pushes universities, especially the ones with a scientific and technological focus, to rethinking their own internal models for organizing, generating and integrating knowledge. The silos centred vision of disciplines born with the Enlightenment, based on a clear separation between organic and inorganic sciences, basic and applied disciplines, sciences and humanities, doesn't seem anymore able to represent contemporary knowledge domains and envision their potential evolution and impacts.

The second factor relates to the transformation of innovation processes themselves and will increasingly challenge technical and scientific universities with the difficult task of reinventing their dynamics to transfer technology and innovation to the outside world. The pressure on universities to take a more active role in the processes of knowledge transfer does not only have to deal with the widening frontiers of knowledge and the foreshadowing of evermore advanced arenas for application. The technological changes described have transformed the processes of innovation themselves and, more explicitly, the methods and dynamics involved in transmitting, recombining and applying knowledge to solve specific problems. Conditions like the exponential growth in access to university education and the

60 Education, research, entrepreneurship, society

hyperconnectivity typical of the digital era mean that knowledge is now more widespread and more approachable (Castells, 1996; Rifkin, 2000). Innovation is evolving from its black box status, conceived by experts hidden away in their R&D departments, to become a much less linear and unidirectional process.

As a consequence, in this rapidly changing world where the frontiers of technology and science are becoming more multi-disciplinary and complex, the model of closed innovation is in decline. In its place is a model where companies join intricate innovation ecosystems where universities' research resources play a key role and can access both internal and external ideas under the banner of open innovation. This model allows actors on the market to tap into an extended network and push their internal innovation, reorganizing their system of relationships through licencing deals, partnerships, mergers and acquisitions. Starting from pioneering initiatives, like Procter & Gamble's "Connect & Develop" launched in 2001, this model has been codified and promoted within strategic company reorganizations. Apart from strategic relationships with external actors, it has led to companies creating proper divisions charged with scouting new ideas that would then be integrated within their processes of innovation via various forms of collaboration (Huston, 2006). This gradually constructed open paradigm is, therefore, system-wide and less locked into the idea of individual "invention", which has started to be questioned within the world of economics and social sciences since the 1980s. Innovation is now seen as the outcome of interrelationships between the economic-productive system and the social system and, ultimately, focuses attention on the role of the users themselves as innovation drivers and contributors (Pinch et al., 1987; Pinch et al., 2005).

As a consequence, both the nature of contemporary technological evolution, characterized by convergent knowledge domains with broad, unexplored and multipurpose applications, as well as the changing dynamics of innovation processes, characterized by an open, participative and multi-stakeholders paradigm, are finally questioning the unique role of technology as an innovation driver.

This is starting to change the very nature of research both in academies and industries in all fields, and putting new disciplines and approaches under the spotlight. More specifically, the aim of better guiding innovation processes towards more meaningful applications, taking into account users and societal centred goals, has led to reconsider a pure tech-driven approach to innovation. Therefore, Design Driven Innovation has seen growing attention both in companies' R&D departments and in universities, especially in the ones leading the science-tech field.[17] Design, bridging by nature science and humanities, is emerging as a powerful lever to guide more meaningful technological innovation. It is a purpose -driven discipline empowered by its culture and user- centered approach, being able to envision new domains of applications (Verganti, 2006; Brown, 2009; Banerjee et al., 2016). This has been leading to an increasing focus on design skills and practices

---

17 In the last ten years major scientific technological universities have been investing in design as a promising discipline for research and education, such as the D-School in Stanford.

within strategic decision-making processes, and on "design thinking", intended as a creative attitude to filter, transfer and connect different bodies of knowledge to envision trajectories of change and drive innovation processes (Martin, 2009; Deserti et al., 2014).

In light of the depicted scenario, a growing pressure on universities to rethink their internal knowledge domains and research processes, as well as their capacity to act as innovation drivers within the open external ecosystem has emerged.

2.3.2 The entrepreneurial university in the ecosystems of innovation

The role held by universities, especially those concentrating on technical and scientific subjects, was thoroughly re-examined in the period overlapping the 20th and 21st centuries, on the back of two factors. The first was the intricate multidisciplinarity typical of Fourth Industrial Revolution innovations, a subject covered previously, and the second factor involved the reconfiguration of the channels used to access and transmit knowledge, following their upheaval during the Digital Revolution. As institutions central to the knowledge economy and increasingly at the heart of mass education processes, universities have certainly contributed towards accelerating several major developments in specific sectors and geographic regions.

In the mid-1980s, a number of technical and scientific research hubs provided a powerful driving force to innovation, among others those linked to the great American universities in the Boston area and to the technical universities around Zurich in German-speaking Switzerland. As the process accelerated over the subsequent two decades, it often led to radical progress in the digital, pharmaceutical and medical domains, as well as in other fields. Initially, these dynamics originated spontaneously through the link between universities and their local production systems, which had been the agents supporting the universities' foundation in the late 19th century and have benefitted from their input ever since. These areas are transformed into true hubs of innovation, which also introduces new entrepreneurship, and are particularly interested in the most pioneering sectors.

Certain other conditions were also met:

- an exponential growth in the number of people with secondary school diplomas and university degrees during the second half of last century
- their constant exposure to technical and scientific fields of application, engendered through stable collaborations with industrial partners scattered across the local area
- the drive towards more advanced levels of education, including research doctorates, with the local business world unable to absorb all these highly trained graduates

These spontaneous dynamics, whereby universities sometimes take on central roles in innovation systems with real development clout, have been observed within studies on development dynamics where the aim is to encode models and so enable them to be replicated. A particular point highlighted is the new way of producing knowledge, which differs from the traditional approaches used in academia. This knowledge is generally elaborated in a practical and not strictly academic setting, it is transdisciplinary rather than subject specific and is heterogeneous rather than homogeneous. From the perspective of the production process, this knowledge often evolves in a non-hierarchical linear manner and is continuously changing and evolving. Instead of being validated by the scientific community, knowledge will run through mechanisms of practical verification and social acceptance within a specific localized setting (Gibbons, 1994).

Many studies use these observations as their starting point to encode models that can explain the processes of innovation at the boundaries between the academic world and the surrounding productive environment. The key feature of this type of innovation is its "systemic" nature – that is to say, it originates within a system where many diverse types of actors exchange ideas, concepts and knowledge, and where the redrawing of boundaries between the subjects themselves is also playing an important part (Castells, 1996; Carayannis et al., 2006). In this context, the models for creating and transmitting knowledge, and knowledge's own capacity to turn into innovation, are tightly linked to relational models and to forms of interaction and involvement, both internal to the academic environment and with external actors (Figure 2.14). We can identify two directions of tension, namely, the relationship ecosystem and the level of integration at which the creation and transmission of knowledge take shape.

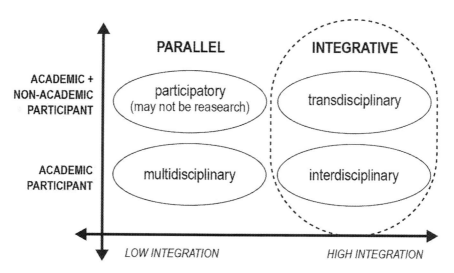

FIGURE 2.14 Models of integration and forms of participation.

Source: Figure extracted from Mauser et al. (2013)

Education, research, entrepreneurship, society **63**

In practice, a model with a high level of integration and a heterogeneous pool of participating actors consists in combining different cognitive and disciplinary approaches and an array of practices, in order to create new knowledge, theories and models which can address the common demand. This approach is based, on the one side, upon the precise logical and methodological framework for each subject. On the other, it can be used to extrapolate the meta-structures that enable a problem to be understood, stimulating the learning models and tools needed to elaborate new applications with a ripple effect, even creating new knowledge within individual subject areas. By contrast, in a model with a low level of integration, knowledge advances in parallel, through logical and methodological frameworks and specialist expertise relating to each subject area, without necessarily delineating inter-system connections or sharing concepts among different contexts or with non-academic actors.

The "system-wide" aspect of innovation is examined more minutely and encoded in models that try to explain the type of different participating actors and their dynamics of interaction. In particular, one of the first models of this kind, the "triple helix" proposed by Henry Etzkowitz and Loet Leydesdorff (1995), adds government agencies and bodies to the subjects involved in innovation systems, alongside universities and companies. The Three Helix model was followed by the authors' own re-elaborations and those of other scholars. These can design complex innovation ecosystems, which also include civil society and the interrelations and impacts of innovation undertakings on the environment. Henry Etzkowitz was particularly concerned with the specific role of universities in qualifying the system of connections between different actors, and he noted the transformations that occur when universities refocus their academic research to include new types of research specifically oriented to technological transfer. He observed the behaviour of several research groups within these systems more closely and, on noting that they were operating with an entrepreneurial mindset, he came up with the term "entrepreneurial university" (Etzkowitz, 2003). With this archetype he represented the innovation systems that emerged spontaneously in certain areas during the transition from the 20th to the 21st century, becoming a reference for many processes of change in universities outside North America, and often guiding policies for the reform of higher education (Kalar & Antoncic, 2015).

But, while this model showed its power as an accelerator for innovation, driving development within certain local areas, it also contains controversial aspects. In many ways, Etzkovitz's entrepreneurial universities, like Stanford and MIT, now look much like proper high-tech businesses, where once it was these types of companies to mirror universities with features such as campuses, working in loosely organized groups, the redefinition of free time and the freedom to organize it (Morozov, 2016). In other words, we have witnessed a gradual capitalizing of universities on the processes of producing knowledge, which has substantially changed the relationship between academia, economic systems and the local communities, sometimes greatly strengthening connections with regional systems (Etzkowitz, 2017). In fact, these new geographies of innovation have certainly spurred

64 Education, research, entrepreneurship, society

knowledge within the local landscape, but have also accentuated inequalities within national economies by draining resources from less attractive areas and creating stiff recessive spirals (Etzkowitz, 2017).

Also, at the global scale, we are assisting to a similar process of polarization of knowledge and innovation capacity. The new world order is characterized by a sort of technological decoupling between geographic regions, especially between China and the United States (Acs, 2004). This gained momentum during the current pandemic with the risks of creating serious discontinuity in the sphere of technological innovation, which could severely alter the global flow of technology, talent and investment. This Sino-American technological decoupling, could potentially expand beyond the strategic sectors at the heart of the conflict between China and the United States (semiconductors, cloud computing, 5G) and reach many other technological domains, seriously disturbing the flow of talent, products, services, capital and investments earmarked for the world of research and innovation.[18] Europe's role and that of its centres for research and innovation must be redrawn in the light of this loaded geopolitical shift, which may cause the greatest upset to globalization since the fall of the Berlin Wall.

Especially in the context of technical and scientific universities, this picture depicted shows that redesigning the system of internal connections (between disciplines) and external relationships (between the many economic, institutional and social actors) can act as a powerful lever to support the processes of innovation, both at local level as well as redefining the balance between global innovation systems. Taking up this challenge, over the past ten years, universities have set up cross-functional facilities as part of their scientific research setup, together with new cognitive and work methods, going beyond the sphere of individual subjects and galvanizing participatory research between universities and external actors, as more effective in generating innovation.

Over time, these knowledge transfer models have reproduced actual business logic and have established academic incubators and accelerators designed with this purpose in mind. A comparative analysis between the various innovation systems in both local and national settings, and the role played by universities in these systems, can help us grasp the new spectrum of possibilities for technical and scientific universities; it also puts the spotlight on their mission's greater critical overview and responsibility within wider local and national strategies.

2.3.3 Entrepreneurial university models balancing opportunities and responsibilities

Taking for granted that the trends presented are global, the different regions, countries and local areas interpret the new model of innovation unevenly to reflect their own social and economic situation, the various systems connecting the actors involved and their greater or lesser capacity to generate innovation within the fields of highest potential impact.

18 https://foreignpolicy.com/2020/05/14/china-us-pandemic-economy-tensions-trump-coronavirus-covid-new-cold-war-economics-the-great-decoupling/

Given the critical importance of technological innovation in underpinning competition within the industrial fabric, the innovation world is also exposing new balances and new competitive landscapes. Starting from that classical indicator of technological innovation, patent submissions, China has risen impressively within the international landscape here as it has for scientific publications, while the United States are more or less stable, and Europe and Japan are clearly in decline (Figure 2.15).

Concentrating on Europe (Figure 2.16), Germany is clearly the engine of European technological innovation with about 10% of all patents lodged in the world but has stumbled somewhat in recent years with innovation newcomer China

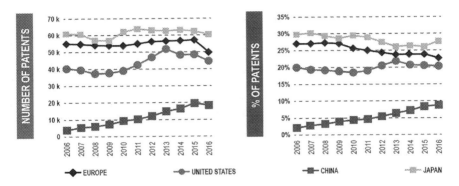

FIGURE 2.15 Number and percentage of patents per geographic region.

Source: OECD – IP5 patent family

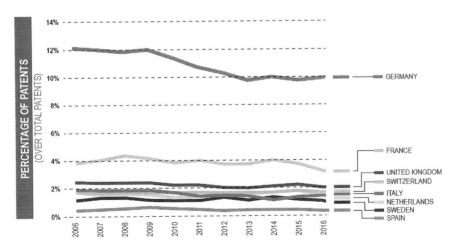

FIGURE 2.16 Percentage of patents on the total of all patents lodged in the world – focus on Europe.

Source: OECD – IP5 patent family

entering the scene. After Germany, comes France (with about 4% of all patents lodged globally) followed by all the other European countries, which contribute with their own smaller quotas of between 2% and 0.5% of all patents submitted. Here also, Europe is presenting a many-actor system, which makes it strong, although there is probably little internal coordination.

Technological innovation, together with all the other facets of impact, has many dimensions and cannot be captured through the number of patents alone. This outlook has spawned many indicators of innovation designed to encapsulate the multi-dimensional impact of innovation on the social and economic fabric of reference. Among these, the *global innovation index* was invented specifically to provide a holistic reading of the process[19] of innovation, condensing together over 30 elements that cover a wide range of input factors and outcomes of innovation (see Figure 2.17).

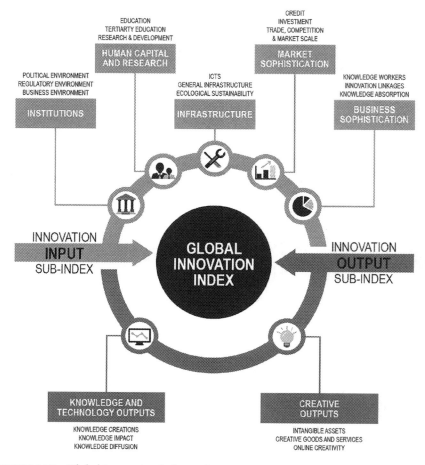

FIGURE 2.17 Global innovation index – elements.

19 www.globalinnovationindex.org/

Education, research, entrepreneurship, society **67**

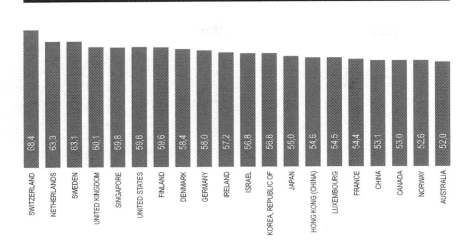

FIGURE 2.18   Global innovation index score 2019 – top 20 countries.

If we observe the world's 20 most innovative countries (see Figure 2.18), as per the global innovation index, Switzerland, the Netherlands and Sweden play an interesting role as economies where the general context (in terms of input factors and results) favours the process of innovation in the local context. Rich countries like Germany, France and even Italy linger behind (in 9th, 16th and 31st place, respectively), showing significant diversification in the model underpinning their economy, probably geared more towards mature products and services than the generation of new business.

Universities in many countries have been engaged in specific actions to stimulate research, with its many dimensions and close-knit links to the industrial fabric, encouraging public–private collaborations and establishing partnerships with leading companies, foundations and other research centres. The EU applied this logic in 2008 when it set up the European Institute of Innovation & Technology (EIT) to strengthen Europe's ability to innovate by promoting university–company alliances,[20] with a focus on finding solutions to the world's most pressing issues. The EIT supports the creation of dynamic, long-term and Europe-wide partnerships among leading companies, research labs and higher education, establishing "communities of innovation", each of which concentrates on researching solutions for a specific global challenge. Since its creation, the EIT has instituted eight communities of innovation (climate, digital, food, health, InnoEnergy, raw materials, manufacturing, urban mobility), plus over 60 innovation hubs across Europe. It has supported over 3,200 new ventures in their start-up and expansion phases, it has generated an external capital of 3.3 billion euros gathered from the subsidized companies. It has led to over 13,000 jobs being created, engaging 3,100

20 European Institute of Innovation & Technology (EIT), eit.europa.eu.

68 Education, research, entrepreneurship, society

graduates with postgraduate or doctoral degrees, and generated over 1,170 new products and services.[21]

In an effort to redraw the system of relationships and play a more effective role in the new system of innovation, individual universities equipped themselves with organizational tools to drive entrepreneurship. They set up internal structures designated to transfer research outcomes with the backing of research groups, enabling them to cash in on their research through patents and licences, start-ups and spin-offs, and through formal collaborations with companies whereby both university and company gained economically from resulting innovations.

In the participatory process of generating and exploiting innovation, universities work alongside start-ups that had originated within their own ecosystem, both in the early stages by providing incubation services and then during their growth acceleration by attracting risk capital; these are key elements that pinpoint the vibrancy present in some universities.

Building start-up incubators/accelerators requires combining efforts in local areas where the conditions are right for creating innovative companies, stimulating the process of open innovation between universities and companies described previously. These facilities, whether created ad hoc or popping up more or less spontaneously, are located in innovation districts, which are zones within a given local area that offer a stimulating environment and a wealth of services, both for the people working there and for the local residents. Alongside the start-ups and spin-offs, multiple laboratories, institutions, co-working spaces and economic actors all set up shop, sharing their know-how and their research.

For innovation districts to thrive, they need:

- a strong bond with the associated university (or universities) and research laboratories
- a network of strong and weak relationships (Granovetter, 1973) between similar and dissimilar actors and among all players in the district
- companies that embrace open innovation, start-ups and spin-offs
- investment funds (venture capital and private equity)[22]

The global diffusion of this model during the past decade means that we can analyse whether the various incubators/accelerators and their technological hubs are more or less able to generate innovation and economic impact. By way of example, UBI Global[23] collects and analyses data in this area. Every year, it publishes a global ranking of incubators and accelerators and has even analysed 1,500+ programmes through a considerable batch of impact indicators.[24]

---

21 European Institute of Innovation & Technology (EIT), data March 2021.
22 Stefano Mainetti, Federica Biancon, PoliHub, https://bit.ly/2PG2q9W.
23 http://ubi-global.com.
24 The UBI Global World Rankings of the Business Incubators and Accelerators, Word Rankings 19/20 Report.

Apart from the detail of the various categories, we can make some general considerations on the data. To start with, the great American universities are absent, despite having been the first to set out the new model of committing to next generation entrepreneurship. The conclusion is that where the model works, it works very well. A lively ecosystem and the actors' natural network have no need for formal structures where the university is involved directly and acts as a guide and mentor. In some way, creating these innovation districts in specific regions, like in Europe, indicates the need to stimulate the system in a more organized way and, in some cases, also the need to involve public institutions as per the wider models already described. The strong European presence, often connected to highly prestigious technical and scientific universities, is joined by China's, where the main features are the size of the accelerators and their local flavour in rapidly developing areas like Beijing, and guidance is not necessarily provided by a single university. Looking at how stimulus can play out, a curious point is the presence of American programmes that are not linked to the great universities but are deployed in areas where there is obviously a general interest in creating innovation to stimulate the economy. Finally, an interesting trend is certainly that of the initiatives originating in the Global South, like those in Africa.

To conclude, in the new model for generating innovation where universities are central to the processes of transformation and stimulating entrepreneurship, the mechanisms for spreading knowledge globally are not yet sufficiently mature for us to elaborate clear frameworks that can point the way for the success of these initiatives. A university's capacity to generate impact does not depend solely on the quality and level of the research that it is able to produce; it is also strongly dependent on the social and economic environment in which the university operates and with which it interacts.

2.4 Universities' role and their projection in society

While universities can certainly contribute significantly to promoting and spreading innovation, society today also expects them to play a major role in circulating good knowledge and to have the capacity to guide and intervene directly in public debate and the design of public policies, especially where complex problems are being addressed. In parallel, universities are urged to drive agendas of diversity, equality and inclusion.

2.4.1 Societal outreach and public engagement: a stronger dialogue between society and universities

Within that broad domain of project-making and experimentation generically labelled as social outreach, there are at least two distinct spheres. One is concerned with the diffusion of knowledge, scientific divulgation, positive contribution to public debate and the design of public policies. The other relates to university involvement in projects with high social value, at different local scales, achieved

70 Education, research, entrepreneurship, society

through public engagement. A major element in both cases is that the various forms of knowledge produced are promoted, exploited and accessed using channels other than the traditional routes of scientific journals and academic learning.

Faced by a tangible loss of trust in institutional sources of knowledge and the propagation of uncontrollable flows of information, we are seeing the unprecedented potential of decentralized production, distribution and diffusion of knowledge. Universities are certainly among the most traditional such sources and have a clear institutional profile within contemporary society. They should, therefore, be able to contribute in different ways to sweeping public debate. In Europe, for example, the European Research Council published its first *ERC Public Engagement with Research Award*[25] in September 2019. This award is designed to recognize ERC grantees who engage with audiences outside their domain to communicate their research, using effective and original means.

In the sphere of public engagement, over the past decades, universities, especially in Europe and North America, have acquired and consolidated new roles within their own local communities. From erstwhile ivory towers, aloft from the daily affairs of cities and urban regions encircling them, they have become proactive actors, open to interacting and working with local authorities, stakeholders and the public, and directly involved in conceiving solutions to the world's woes that are both technically pertinent and socially appropriate. Many universities are now becoming involved in global matters, from a perspective of international cooperation.

When we look at their contribution to public debate, universities mostly concentrate on spreading scientific knowledge through the work of their teaching staff, who write popular science texts and speak at public meetings, outdoor fairs and open seminars. When instead we look at public engagement, the potential options are quite varied. The list includes designing and implementing public interest programmes and projects, building initiatives in collaboration with other bodies for urban development or to benefit the local area, as well as initiatives that involve the public directly, along with other actors, in debates and shared decisions concerning the local community and area.

In Italy, after the initial attempts to create a countrywide system and identify the areas of recurring activity, a network of universities involved in public engagement matters[26] proposed a first analysis matrix that can be applied to the work carried out by universities. Among the items mentioned are:

- *public engagement included in the universities' mission*, strategic guidelines and communications, its integration with other missions and its appreciation within the academic community

---

25 https://erc.europa.eu/news/erc-public-engagement-with-research-award-launched
26 APENET, a network of universities and research centres that works in a participatory manner to promote the planning and exploitation of innovative tools and actions to encourage cultural change in Italy, and which supports institutionalized public engagement www.apenetwork.it.

Education, research, entrepreneurship, society **71**

- *level of awareness* about public engagement matters within the upper echelons of universities and departments, ambassadors present within the academic community, and the university's involvement in national and international networks
- *overview*, in each university, of the level to which its public engagement initiatives are institutionalized and backed by coordination and support structures, and the level of involvement, training, and updating among its staff and students
- *public engagement* included in evaluation processes and among recruitment and career progression criteria, and monitoring the staff's and students' commitment in this field

Several interesting forms of public engagement have been trialled internationally in recent years. For example, in the United Kingdom, the *National Co-ordinating Centre for Public Engagement*[27] (NCCPE) has been operating since 2008. NCCPE's primary function is inspiring and supporting universities to engage with the public. NCCPE identifies and spreads good practices and acts as a training centre for universities interested in building a solid relationship with society, operating through channels of communication and divulgation, as well as by directly involving many different types of actors. Other similar initiatives include first-hand involvement in urban planning, such as with the *Coalition of Urban Serving Universities*[28] (USU), a network of public urban research centres which was founded in 2005 in the United States. USU sets itself on the mission to be a meeting point between the intellectual capital of urban universities and urban environments, especially the most marginal and disadvantaged areas and, through research and education, help to build policies that can improve urban life.

Politecnico di Milano is also committed to a wide range of outreach programmes; several have been running for many years, while others are more recent, confirming the fact that the two traditional cornerstones of academic work (teaching and research) are joined by social engagement and cooperation towards development, pointing the university towards a model of responsible research.

A facility that stands out in particular for its commitment to spreading knowledge is Hoc-Lab,[29] an interdisciplinary laboratory at the Department of Electronics, Information and Bioengineering specializing in multimedia communication. Another is the FDS Laboratory[30] at the Department of Mathematics, which acts as a bridge between the university and schools, designing

27 www.publicengagement.ac.uk
28 https://usucoalition.org
29 http://hoc.elet.polimi.it/hoc
30 http://effediesse.mate.polimi.it/?lg=it

and implementing initiatives to consolidate the students' learning, as well as advanced education for their professors, experimental teaching and pre-university advisory services.

If we look at initiatives that have a more direct social value, one of the most consolidated programmes, Polisocial,[31] has been engaged in various forms of responsible research for a number of years. Polisocial promotes "a new form of multi-disciplinary project planning that cares about human and social development, expanding opportunities for education, research and exchange programmes for students, young researchers, teaching staff and technical and administrative personnel within the university and its network". The initiatives supported by Polisocial are enacted through the agency of development aid, where technical cooperation is at the service of local autonomous development, thereby creating opportunities for experimentation and field research in non-conventional international fields, as well as through the *Polisocial Award*. The scheme finances research projects with a social purpose conducted at Politecnico di Milano, funded through pre-tax donations to Politecnico di Milano.[32] Figure 2.19 gives a flavour of some of PoliHub's initiatives.

FIGURE 2.19 Polisocial award: Politecnico di Milano's programme for commitment to social responsibility. Several funded projects.

31 www.polisocial.polimi.it/it/home/
32 *When taxpayers in Italy complete their tax return, they can allocate a quota of five per thousand of tax due to a preferred organisation included in the directory of approved organizations.*

Education, research, entrepreneurship, society **73**

> Off campus, "Il Cantiere per le Periferie" (*a building site for the city's out-skirts*), is a project designed to strengthen the presence of Politecnico di Milano in the city, by setting up local spaces where professors, researchers and students develop initiatives in experimental teaching, responsible research and co-design with local organizations, creating a virtuous circle.
>
> Various projects run under the banner of "Didattica sul Campo" (*on-field teaching*) establish a link between the university's teaching and training programmes and the requests emerging from local areas and communities.

2.4.2 Diversity, equality and inclusion

Within the universities themselves, diversity, equality and inclusion are other fundamental steps in the process to generate innovation and construct open and democratic knowledge. Universities that intend to maintain high standards of excellence and technological innovation must be able to attract talented people at all levels and be unequivocally open to diversity across the board, from study paths and behaviour to background, origin and career opportunities.

Universities that are able to pursue and engage in policies that favour inclusion, for students and staff alike, will expand the value of their mission of teaching and research and re-enforce its message (Milem et al., 2005; Fine et al., 2010).

In the same way, it is challenging for single universities to engage in inclusion policies as a way of mitigating current imbalances affecting students, staff and society in general, with inclusion now often featuring heavily in global policies. Across Europe, universities are implementing institutional policies for diversity, equality and inclusion.[33] The internationalization of higher education and research, in combination with student and staff mobility, are at the basis of understanding, appreciating and integrating diversities. By the same token, equality between women and men, one of the European Union's founding values, is and has been at the centre of broad-spectrum policies, including in education, research and innovation.

The European Commission's Horizon 2020 programme has been elaborating its triennial report *She Figures* since 2003; based on a large set of indicators, it gives a picture of the progress in equality between women and men in education, research and innovation within Europe, and the effectiveness of policies implemented to drive this agenda. The recent *She Figures 2018*[34] indicate that the impact of these policies is substantially positive, highlighting the need for further effort if true equality is to be reached over the next few years. *She Figures 2018* shows that, on average, there is a broad gender balance at master's and PhD levels. However, gender distribution in the different scientific fields of study is uneven, stressing the

---

33 Michael Murphy, European University Association (EUA 2018).

34 She Figures 2018, European Commission 2019, Directorate-General for Research and Innovation. Horizon 2020 Science with and for Society. https://ec.europa.eu/info/publications/she-figures-2018_en.

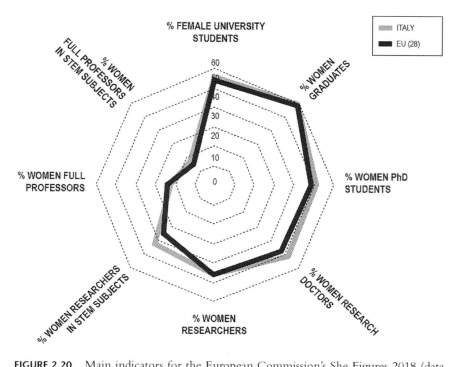

FIGURE 2.20 Main indicators for the European Commission's She Figures 2018 (data 2016). The gender-disaggregated statistics show whether implemented policies are efficient and help to design measures for mitigating inequalities based on gender. Data re-elaborated from She Figures 2018.[35]

persistence of gender stereotypes, especially strong in the fields of science, technology, engineering and mathematics (STEM subjects).

Women remain underrepresented in academia, and still make up the minority of top academic positions (see Figure 2.20). While Italy falls in line with the EU average, there are strong inequalities in STEM subjects in general and, for the purposes of our study, in the opportunities for women to access top academic positions. This is clear if we look at the *glass ceiling index (GCI)* in a university setting, which provides a concise indicator to compare the quota of women in the academic world (working as researchers, associate and full professors, or equivalent) against the quota of women holding the highest academic positions (positions equivalent to full professor in most European universities). The GCI is inversely proportional to female representation and the possibility of women accessing high profile academic positions (see Figure 2.21). If we take Italy as a whole, several universities, including Politecnico di Milano, have compiled gender mainstreaming reports, giving

[35] https://op.europa.eu/en/publication-detail/-/publication/9540ffa1-4478-11e9-a8ed-01aa75ed71a1/language-en

Education, research, entrepreneurship, society 75

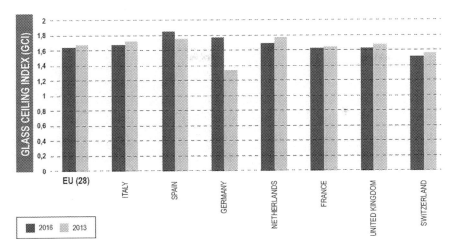

FIGURE 2.21 Glass ceiling index (GCI) in an academic setting, 2013–2016 for a group of European countries. Data re-elaborated from the EU's She Figures 2018.

a snapshot of the situation and tools to design policies to reduce the gender gap. A recent report on the topic (Pacchi, 2020) noted that, just in Italy, 36% of people studying for a STEM subject degree are women, while women make up 62.4% of all those studying for a degree in a non-STEM subject. This gap is even greater if the analysis is restricted to Milan-based universities, where women make up 30% of the total in studying STEM subjects but 62.6% in non-STEM degree courses.

In this panorama of inequality that is far from being bridged, the Covid-19 pandemic put a spotlight on today's social challenges and opportunities, especially in education and research. There is, on the one side, a real risk that the pandemic could acerbate existing social inequalities; as one but not the only example, think of the difficult balance between professional and private lives, with all the repercussions on women's careers. On the other, the totally unprecedented situation is a good opportunity to set out long-term strategies, where the objective of mitigating imbalances and today's social divide can be a defining moment within planning and policymaking.

Chapter references

Acs, Z. J. (2004). Innovation and the growth of cities. In *Contributions to economic analysis* (Vol. 266, pp. 635–658). Cheltenham, UK and Northampton, MA: Elsevier.
Amari, S. (1977). Neural theory of association and concept-formation. *Biological Cybernetics* 26, 175–185.
Amit, D. J. (1989). *Modeling brain function*. Cambridge: Cambridge University Press.
Baker, D. P. (2008). Privatization, mass higher education, and the super research university. Symbiotic or zero-sum trends? *Journal für Wissenschaft und Bildung, 17*(2), 36–52.

76 Education, research, entrepreneurship, society

Baker, D. P. (2018). *The schooled society. The educational transformation of global culture*. San Francisco, CA: Stanford University Press.

Banerjee, B., & Ceri, S. (Eds.). (2016). *Creating innovation leaders. A global perspective*. Switzerland: Springer International Publishing.

Bonaiuti G., Calvani A., Menichetti L., & Vivanet G. (2017). *Le tecnologie educative*. Roma: Carocci editore.

Brown, T. (2009). *Change by design: How design thinking transforms organizations and inspires innovation*. New York, NY: Harper Collins.

Bucchi, M. (2004). *Science in society: An introduction to social studies of science*. London and New York, NY: Routledge.

Calvani, A. (2009). *Teorie dell'istruzione e carico cognitivo*. Trento, Italy: Erickson.

Carayannis, E. G., & Campbell, D. F. J. (Eds.). (2006). *Knowledge creation, diffusion, and use in innovation networks and knowledge clusters: A comparative systems approach across the United States, Europe, and Asia*. London: Greenwood.

Castells, M. (1996). The rise of the network society. In *The information age. Economy, society and culture, Vol. 1 (of a book trilogy)*. Malden, MA and Oxford: Blackwell Publishers.

Clark, B. R. (1998). The entrepreneurial university: Demand and response. *Tertiary Education and Management, 4*(1), 5–16.

Cuseo Joseph, B. (1997). *Cooperative learning: A pedagogy for addressing contemporary challenges and critical issues in higher education*. Stillwater, OK: New Forums Press.

Cyranoski, D., Gilbert, N., Ledford, H., Nayar, A., & Yahia, M. (2011). *Education: The PhD factory*. Nature.com.

De Martin, J. C. (2016). *Università futura: Tra democrazia e bit*. Torino, Italy: Codice Edizioni.

Deserti, A., & Rizzo, F. (2014). Design and the cultures of enterprises. *Design Issue, 30*(1), 36–56.

Drucker, P. F. (2011). *The age of discontinuity: Guidelines to our changing society*. Transaction Publishers, Butterworth-Heinemann.

Etzkowitz, H. (2003). Research groups as 'quasi-firms': The invention of the entrepreneurial university. *Research Policy, 32*(1), 109–121.

Etzkowitz, H. (2017). Innovation lodestar: The entrepreneurial university in a stellar knowledge firmament. In *Technological forecasting & social change*. New York, NY: Elsevier.

Etzkowitz, H., & Leydesdorff, L. (1995). The triple helix – university-industry-government relations: A laboratory for knowledge based economic development. *EASST Review, 14*, 14–19.

Etzkowitz, H., & Leydesdorff, L. (2000). The dynamics of innovation: From national systems and 'Mode 2' to a triple helix of university – industry – government relations. *Research Policy, 29*(2), 109–123.

Fine, E., & Handelsman, J. (2010). *Benefits and challenges of diversity in academic settings*. Brochure prepared for the Women in Science & Engineering Leadership Institute (WISELI). University of Wisconsin.

Freeman, F. C., & Soete, L. (2004). *The economics of industrial innovation* (3rd ed.). London and New York, NY: Routledge.

Gibbons M., Limoges C., Nowotny H., Schwartzman S., Scott P., & Trow M. (1994). *The new production of knowledge*. London: SAGE.

Graham, R. (2018). *The global state of the art in engineering education*. Cambridge, MA: MIT Press.

Granovetter, M. S. (1973). The strength of weak ties. *American Journal of Sociology, 78*(6), 1360–1380.

Grebenshchikova, E. (2016). NBIC-convergence and technoethics: Common ethical perspective. *International Journal of Technoethics, 7*(1), 77–84.

Grilli, E. (2005). *Crescita e sviluppo delle Nazioni. Teorie, strategie e risultati*. Milan, Italy: UTET Università.

Hansen, M. T., & Birkinshaw, J. (2006). The innovation value chain. *Harvard Business Review*.

Harari, Y. N. (2017). *Homo Deus. Breve storia del futuro*. Milano, Italy: Bompiani.

Hopfield, J. J. (1982). Neural networks and physical systems with emergent collective computational abilities. *Biophysics, 79*, 2554–2558.

Huston, L., & Sakkab, N. (2006). Connect and develop: Inside Procter & Gamble's new model for innovation. *Harvard Business Review*, 58–66.

Jencks, C., & Riesman, D. (1968). *The academic revolution*. New York, NY: Doubleday.

Kahneman, D. (2011). *Thinking, fast and slow*. New York, NY: Farrar, Straus and Giroux.

Kalar, B., & Antoncic, B. (2015). The entrepreneurial university, academic activities and technology and knowledge transfer in four European countries. *Technovation, 36*, 1–11.

Khushf, J. (2007). The ethics of NBIC convergence. *Journal of Medicine and Philosophy, 32*(3), 185–196.

Kline, R. R. (2015). *The cybernetics moment: Or why we call our age the information age*. John Baltimore, MD: Hopkins University Press.

Kolko, J. (2015). *Design thinking comes of age*. Cambridge: Harvard Business Review.

Kurtweil, R. (2013). *How to create a mind: The secret of human thought revealed*. New York, NY: Penguin Book.

Loverige, D., Dewick, P., & Randles, S. (2008). Converging technologies at the nano-scale: The making of a new world? *Technology Analysis and Strategic Management, 20*(1), 29–43.

Martin, R., & Martin, R. L. (2009). *The design of business: Why design thinking is the next competitive advantage*. Cambridge, MA: Harvard Business Press.

Marzano, F. (2008). *Economia della crescita. Dalla teoria classica alle controversie fra contemporanei*. Milan: Mondadori Università.

Mauser W., et al. (2013). Transdisciplinary global change research: the co-creation of knowledge for sustainability, Volume 5, Issues 3–4, Pages 420-431.

Milem, J. F., Chang, M. J., & Antonio, A. L. (2005). *Making diversity work on campus: A research-based perspective*. Washington, DC: Association American Colleges and Universities.

Mitchell, M. (2019). *Artificial intelligence. A guide for thinking humans*. USA: Farrar, Straus and Giroux.

Montedoro, L., & Pasqui, G. (2020). Università e cultura. Una scissione inevitabile? Milano, Italy: Maggioli.

Morozov, E. (2016). *Silicon Valley. I signori del silicio* (Italian edition). Torino, Italy: Codice Edizioni.

Pacchi, C., & Parma, A. (2020). Le ragazze di fronte alla formazione scientifica e tecnologica: sfide e strategie a Milano. *Rapporto Ambrosianeum*.

Pinch, T., & Oudshoorn, N. (2005). *How users matter: The co-construction of users and technology*. Cambridge, MA: MIT Press.

Pinch, T., Bijker, W. E., & Hughes, T. P. (1987). *The social construction of technological systems: New directions in the sociology and history of technology*. Cambridge, MA: MIT Press.

Quinn, J. B. (1992). *Intelligent enterprise. A knowledge and service based paradigm for industry*. New York, NY: The Free Press.

Rifkin, J. (2000). *Age of access: The new culture of hypercapitalism*. Penguin, Pacific University.

Tress, B. et al. (2006). From landscape research to landscape planning: Aspects of integration, education and application. Springer, Dordrecht, The Netherlands.

3
GOVERNANCE IN UNIVERSITIES

To gain a clear understanding of the governance in university systems, we first need to look at the paradigms for university–state interaction, and then go down a level to examine the various ways individual universities govern themselves. While there are institutional, political and economic features specific to each country, we can see some Europe-wide tendencies.

Starting from the studies by Baldridge (1971) and Clark (1983), the three main governance models explored in the literature on university governance and university–state relationships are faculty self-governance, state control, and the market model. The actual names can be slightly different: "in Clark's model (1983), the three possible types of relationships between the state and the universities are: control by the state, free market, and administration of the universities carried out by 'academic oligarchies' (self-regulation)" (Agasisti et al., 2006).

The models described are naturally ideal types, given that in reality there are many hybrid configurations that can define a particular stage in a national setting or contexts with more than one model (as is the case today in the United Kingdom).

In the words of Bleiklie and Kogan (2007):

> *professional self-regulation under which academics independently run their research and teaching operations, representative democracy that grants participatory rights to staff and students in institutional decision-making processes, bureaucratic steering by which the state regulates publicly funded educational institutions and corporate management as a means to render higher education institutions efficient and accountable – are not mutually exclusive.*

3.1 Interaction between university and government

In general, the model where a university is self-governed by its faculty was the first to have developed in the modern age, and it can be related, without

DOI: 10.4324/9781003231004-04

overlapping perfectly, to the Humboldtian model of higher education, exemplified in the foundation of the University of Berlin (today Humboldt University of Berlin) in the early 19th century. Humboldt's ideal is a holistic combination of teaching and research, independence from outside economic and social constraints and the need to produce results that could be "applied", and independence from within with free choice in teaching and learning (Lehrfreiheit and Lernfreiheit) and education to instruct citizens instead of providing skills for the job market (Rider, 2009).

From the mid-19th century, several types of universities shifted away from the concept of a distinct separation between university and local economy set out in the Humboldtian model. Among these are the land-granted universities in the United States and the technical universities of France first and Italy later (Gherardini, 2015). All these universities focused on training technical profiles in the foremost sectors of the local economy, during the First and Second Industrial Revolutions and, that aside, in farming; they were also keen to produce applied research directed towards system-wide innovation, albeit often in incremental stages.

In the second half of the 20th century, the model for managing European universities gradually detached itself from the ideal of self-governance, to introduce arrangements where the state took more control, a process that played out more or less intensely in the different countries; see, for example, the introduction of university accreditation systems (Capano et al., 2015).

Starting in the 1990s, many western countries facing major changes to their economies (de-industrialization, post-Fordism, greater emphasis on knowledge as a factor of production) and local society (lengthening of studies and significant rise in number of students) embarked upon reforming their universities. The outcome of these reforms was to distance universities from the traditional self-governance model and from direct state control (Capano et al., 2015).

A shared vision began to gain purchase during this stage, where the intention was to move from the model of state-controlled universities to a hybrid model, inspired by the British local autonomy model, with oversight and control mechanisms over the results (*steering at a distance*) and via the market (universities competing for resources). The guidelines for this model are to give the universities their institutional independence, evaluate the quality of teaching and research that individual universities can provide as autonomous institutions, and the introduction of competitive forms of financing that reward or penalize universities on the basis of their results.

In general, the transformations caused by reforms do not bring up any clear outcome in favour of abandoning the state-controlled model for a market model. It rather points towards a hybrid approach, drawing, as mentioned, on the *new public management* model, first introduced by academics in the United Kingdom and Australia. The greater autonomy (for statutes, finances, etc.) and the incentive of competition among the system's actors are joined by an apparatus of state evaluation and control, used by the state to allocate resources (ordinary and performance-based rewards).

80 Governance in universities

3.2 University governance models

The evolution of state-level university governance systems was joined by an ever-cleaner break from the model of internal self-governance, with collegiate bodies beginning to lose their importance in favour of more vertical and centralized models.

During the 1990s, many European countries embarked on reforms in higher education, directed in essence towards establishing more vertical decisional processes. Today, in Europe, we can identify two macro-archetypes of governance structure (Bennetot et al., 2017):

- *Unitary governance structure*, referring to structures of governance where a single body exercises decisional powers. This can have features proper of an academic senate or typical of a board of directors.
- *Dual governance structure*, typically consisting of a board (or committee) and an academic senate, potentially chaired by different people. While the terminology varies considerably from country to country, the senate is often a large representative body, which includes the academic community and, to a greater or lesser extent, other categories of university staff, while the board/committee is generally smaller but can include people from outside the university. The expertise and sharing of duties among the governance bodies are clearly split between the board/committee and the senate, but the partitioning itself can vary markedly from country to country.

The dual governance structure is split into two further sub-archetypes:

1 *Dual governance structure – traditional model*, where the board/committee is typically responsible for long-term strategic decisions (statutes, strategic plans, budget selection and allocation), while the academic senate, consisting mainly of members within the university community, is instead in charge of academic matters (curricula and qualifications, and staff career progression)
2 *Dual governance structure – asymmetric model*, where one of the two bodies is the main decisional body, and the other has a more limited scope and is generally in an advisory capacity

An overview of the geographic distribution for these governance archetypes in Europe is shown in Figure 3.1.

Most reforms in higher education governance introduced in Europe were inspired by the principle of institutional autonomy, meant as the capacity of each university to determine how it runs itself, its own organization and management, it can decide its priorities and manage its finances, it can prepare its own recruitment policies and decide what it includes in its programmes and courses; see Figure 3.2 for a concise analysis of several indicators in a few European countries.

In line with the European process, the 2010 reform in the Italian system was designed to streamline the universities' governance arrangements by introducing a

Governance in universities **81**

FIGURE 3.1 Geographic distribution of governance macro models.

Source: Bennetot, P.E. and Estermann T. (2017), University Autonomy in Europe III: The scorecard 2017. EUA European University Association

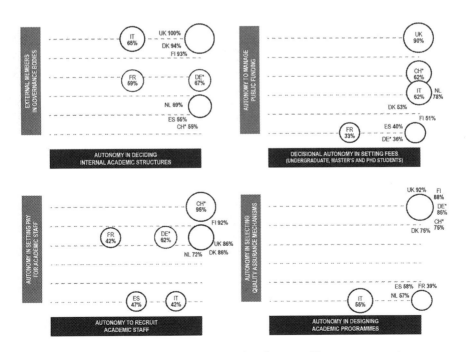

FIGURE 3.2 University autonomy: a comparison between European countries.

Source: Data from Bennetot, P.E. and Estermann T. (2017), University Autonomy in Europe III: The scorecard 2017. EUA European University Association

82 Governance in universities

vertical governance structure, inspired by principles of organizational simplification. The reform, which was then implemented, abolished the matrix form of organization. In its classic declination, this matrix was based on two different types of organizational units, one overseeing research processes (e.g. research departments) and the other overseeing education processes (e.g. schools).

The new form of governance has reduced the average number of departments and cross-functional bodies (e.g. schools) compared to the previous situation (Figure 3.3).

The dual "traditional" governance model used in British universities was introduced in Italy after the 2010 reform. Nevertheless, there are significant differences in institutional autonomy and internal organization, determining widely dissimilar levels and degrees of independence. The profiles of four European universities are given in the following, as examples of the four governance systems. TU Belin represents the typical unitary governance model in Germany, University College London (UCL) represents the dual "traditional" model in England, while Politecnico di Milano portrays the dual "traditional" model in Italy, but with lesser autonomy. TU Delft exemplifies the dual "asymmetric" model in the Netherlands.

These four universities are compared against similar universities in Table 3.1. The table includes data about faculty and students to give a clear picture of each university. The ratio between junior faculty plus PhD students and tenured faculty brings up noticeable differences from system to system. In the two German universities, for example, this ratio is between 9 and 18. In Switzerland, the situation is

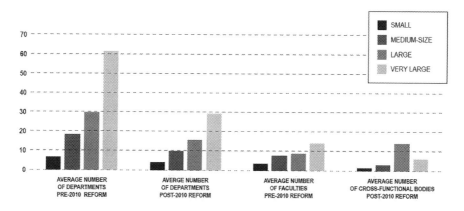

FIGURE 3.3 Italian universities: average number of structures (departments, faculties, schools) pre- and post-2010 reform compared to university size. Size N of university calculated on the basis of students in the academic year 2011/2012. Small university: $N < 10,000$; medium-sized university: $10,000 < N < 20,000$; large university: $20,000 < N < 40,000$; very large university: $N > 40,000$.

Source: Data from Capano and Regini (Eds.) (2015), Come cambia la governance. Università italiane ed europee a confronto, Fondazione Crui

Governance in universities   **83**

TABLE 3.1 Organizational chart for several European universities collected from official data published on their websites for 2019.

	Tenured Faculty (nos.)	Students (nos.)	Junior Faculty / Tenured Faculty	PhD / Tenured Faculty	(Junior Faculty + PhD) / Tenured Faculty	Students / Total Faculty
TU Berlin	497	34,000	5.3	4.1	9.4	10.9
RWTH Aachen	547	45,000	10.2	8.2	18.4	7.4
UCL	2,860	38,300	1.7	3.5	5.2	4.9
Imperial College	1,243	17,600	2.0	3.4	5.4	4.7
ETH	481	19,800	12.1	8.3	20.4	3.2
EPFL	318	10,500	10.8	6.6	17.4	2.8
PoliMI	1,320	45,000	0.7	0.8	1.5	19.8
CentraleSupélec	370	5,000	0.4	1.1	1.5	9.3
TU Delft	951	23,400	1.0	3.2	4.2	12.6
Chalmers	530	11,000	1.7	2.0	3.7	7.6

similar, with up to 20 assistants for each faculty member. UCL and Imperial College, with their dual governance model and high level of independence, operate at about five. In other European countries, the leverage ratio is generally less than five. The difference in the number of students and professors is also reflected clearly in the student-faculty ratio, and thus impacting on the service level in education.

These differences in organization, rather than depending on the different governance models, seem instead to depend on the type of academic career in the country and the relative status of university teaching staff.

TU Berlin

Structure and organizational autonomy

- The governance model is based on an extended academic senate, academic senate and executive board.
- The extended academic senate is an elected body that is representative of the university internally; its functions are to elect the executive board members and draw up changes to the university statute.
- The executive board is responsible for managing the university in its entirety.
- The academic senate is a subgroup of the extended academic senate and it validates all the decisions proposed by the executive board.
- A number of committees headed by elected senate members protect the interests of the various groups of people within the organization.
- Organizationally, the university is structured into faculties.

84 Governance in universities

Status and staff recruitment

- Teaching staff and most technical and administrative staff are defined as public-sector employees.
- The overall number of new places open for academic and administrative staff, and salary levels, are set by the faculties on the basis of development plans and available funding and must be run past the academic senate.

Academic and financial autonomy

- Total number of students (undergraduate and master's) and admission criteria are defined internally. Faculties propose the content of current programmes and the activation of new ones (undergraduate and post-graduate, including at PhD level) to the academic senate for approval.
- Public funding is regulated on an annual basis by the appropriate minister, although the university has significant freedom in matters of private financing.
- By law, students pay no tuition fees.

UCL

Structure and organizational autonomy

- UCL's governance structure includes the council, the academic board and a formal committee structure. The council is UCL's governing body and academic board its senior academic authority. The operational management of UCL is the responsibility of the Provost's senior management team (SMT).
- As UCL's governing body, the council oversees the management and administration of UCL and the conduct of its affairs, subject to the advice of the academic board on matters of academic policy. The council approves UCL's mission and strategic vision and its long-term academic and business plans. The council delegates authority to the Provost, as chief executive, for the academic, corporate, financial, estate and human resources management of UCL. The council normally meets six times each year.
- The university defines its governance structure internally, within the guidelines set in the "Higher Education Code of Governance".
- The university can define its organizational structure internally.
- Organizationally, the university is structured into schools, and in general they have significant independence.

Governance in universities 85

Status and staff recruitment

- Teaching staff and technical and administrative staff do not have a civil servant status.
- The university has complete freedom to define its recruitment and promotion policies for teaching and administrative staff.
- Pay and grading (salary bands) for teaching staff are negotiated with the support of external authorities through national pay frameworks.
- The university decides the pay and grading for administrative staff independently.

Academic and financial autonomy

- Financing is regulated on a yearly basis by the government, and the university has no restrictions on how public funding is used.
- The university sets its own selection and admission criteria at undergraduate and master's levels internally.
- British undergraduate students pay tuition fees which are determined internally up to a maximum set by the government, and the university is free to set its tuition fees for postgraduate students.
- The university can set its tuition fees for international students (undergraduate and postgraduate) outside the EU or EEA. From 2021 to 2022, most EU and EEA students will be charged international student fees.
- The university manages course content at all levels as well as the activation of new programmes independently.
- The university must meet criteria set by the Quality Assurance Agency for Higher Education.

Politecnico di Milano

Structure and organizational autonomy

- The governance model is based on an academic senate and board of Directors (dual governance model).
- The academic senate is an elected body that is representative of the university internally; it directs and programmes the university's development, especially in teaching and research.
- The board of directors oversees the university's strategies and has legislative functions, as well as directing and controlling the university's administrative, economic and asset management. It includes external directors.

86 Governance in universities

- The organizational structure (departments and liaison commissions) must comply with legal constraints.
- The rector is elected and remains in office for a single non-renewable six-year mandate.

Status and staff recruitment

- Teaching staff and most technical and administrative staff are defined as public-sector employees.
- The overall number of new positions for academic and administrative staff, and the promotion system, is regulated through public competitions. Pay is set by an external authority.

Academic and financial autonomy

- Total number of students (undergraduate and master's) and admission criteria are defined internally. The content of current programmes and activation of new ones (undergraduate and postgraduate, including at PhD level) must go through an accreditation process.
- Public funding is regulated on an annual basis by the appropriate minister, although the university has significant freedom in matters of private financing.
- Tuition fees paid by students are determined internally. However, the total amount of tuition fees paid by Italian and EU students cannot be more than 20% of the university's public funding.

TU Delft

Structure and organizational autonomy

- The governance structure is based on a dual "asymmetric" model, with an executive board and a number of consultation bodies (established by law).
- The executive board consists of a president and vice-president, appointed by and responding to the supervisory board, whose members are appointed by the appropriate ministry.
- The executive board is the main decisional body and is responsible for strategic and financial decisions, and personnel management. However, it must gain the backing of the main consultation bodies, including the General Assembly of Councils, which has the right of veto in several decisional areas.
- Its organizational structure is defined internally.

Governance in universities **87**

Status and staff recruitment

- Teaching staff and technical and administrative staff are defined as public-sector employees.
- The university has complete freedom to define its recruitment and promotion policies for academic and administrative staff.
- Staff salary bands are negotiated between the national rectors' conference and the relevant trade unions.

Academic and financial autonomy

- Public funding is regulated on an annual basis by the appropriate minister, although the university has significant freedom in matters of private financing.
- Admission to undergraduate and masters' courses is basically free (with some exceptions). Student selection (undergraduate and master's) is regulated jointly by the university and the ministry; the university can set additional criteria for master's students.
- The university is independent in its management of course content at all levels, as well as in activating new programmes. However, any new undergraduate or master's programme must be accredited by the National Advisory Council.
- Undergraduate and master's students pay tuition fees, which is determined by the Ministry for Dutch plus EU/EFTA (and Surinamese) students, while the university is free to set its tuition fees for postgraduate students. The university can set its tuition fees for international students (undergraduate and postgraduate) outside the EU and EFTA.

Chapter references

Agasisti, T., & Catalano, G. (2006). Governance models of university systems – Towards quasi-markets? Tendencies and perspectives: A European comparison. *Journal of Higher Education Policy and Management, 28*(3), 245–262, 248.

Baldridge, J. V. (1971). *Power and conflict in the university: Research in the sociology of complex organizations.* New York, NY: John Wiley.

Bennetot, P. E., & Estermann, T. (2017). *University autonomy in Europe III: The scorecard 2017.* EUA European University Association. www.university-autonomy.eu

Bleiklie, I., & Kogan, M. (2007). Organization and governance of universities. *Higher Education Policy, 20*, 477–493, 479.

Capano, G., & Regini, M. (Eds.). (2015). *Come cambia la governance. Università italiane ed europee a confronto.* Rome: Fondazione Crui.

Clark, B. R. (1983). *The higher education system: Academic organizations in cross national perspective.* Berkeley, CA: University of California Press.

88 Governance in universities

Gherardini, A. (2015). *Squarci nell'avorio: le università italiane e l'innovazione economica.* Florence: Firenze University Press.

Rider, S. (2009). The future of the European University: Liberal democracy or authoritarian capitalism? *Culture Unbound, 1,* 83–104.

4

STRATEGIC CHOICES FOR UNIVERSITIES OF SCIENCE AND TECHNOLOGY

The final section of this text opens the door to new horizons. We will look to the future, and we will try and define the elements that can guide choices that technical universities must face.

We have reached this point in our trail of investigations and interpretations, having started from the analysis of the four elements that compose universities, which we examined, and then we covered relatively consolidated models, such as *education, research, entrepreneurial innovation* and *social outreach*. However, looking at the challenges thrown up by the social and economic landscape, as well as by scientific and technological progress, the university world is facing choices that must be taken from within a new framework of reference.

We are therefore proposing to reformulate the strategic predicaments that universities will come up against in the future along three *axes* instead, according to what universities do. Our three axes are knowledge, relationships and system. We can move around in our new framework, ask key questions when planning a path of evolution and detect the possible answers. Each will offer benefits and disadvantages, and the weight of either will depend on the context specific to each university.

The first axis expresses the strategies and modalities to generate, transmit, communicate and cross-fertilize knowledge. We are shifting from an essentially vertical and subject-specific approach to a more horizontal master plan that sweeps across the boundaries separating disciplines, and matters are organized starting from the questions and problems.

The second axis, relationships, examines the importance of the various relationship systems that universities slot into (and, on a smaller scale, the single researchers and professors). The purpose is to identify the potential threats and benefits of strategies based on competitions and empowering individual universities, professors

DOI: 10.4324/9781003231004-05

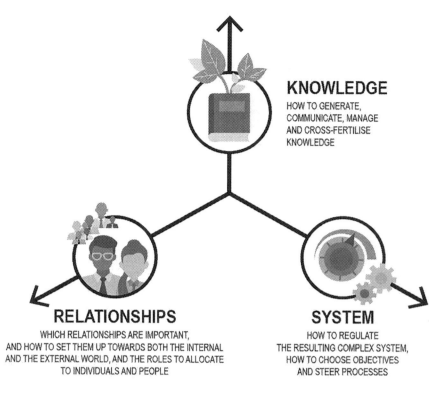

FIGURE 4.1 Domains where tomorrow's strategies will be played out.

and researchers, instead of strategies based on empowering networks to improve and enrich teaching and research.

The axis of knowledge, which is concerned with "what" universities do, and the axis of relationships, which is concerned with "who" does what in universities, are enabled by the third axis, system, which is concerned with "how" universities are run, that is, the governance models in the single universities and in the overall university system whereby the choices along the first two axes are both possible and feasible.

There are crossroads in the path of each of these three elements, and we will explore the potential choices and implications. In some cases, choices are based on polarity, and one choice will automatically exclude the other. Other times, the two poles are at either end of a continuum, and sometimes elements facing apparently opposite directions can coexist or be combined.

4.1 Knowledge – its forms, objectives and how it develops

Given their central role, the creation of a Europe of knowledge is for the universities a source of opportunity, but also of major challenges. Indeed, universities go about their business in an increasingly globalised environment which is constantly

Strategic choices for universities of science and technology **91**

changing and is characterised by increasing competition to attract and retain outstanding talent and by the emergence of new requirements for which they have to cater.[36]

In the context of "knowledge-based economy and society", we are witnessing an increasing evolution to our framework of reference, with new markets, new actors and new "knowledge-intensive" activities propounding to guide development and management in information and knowledge. Creating knowledge goes hand-in-hand with creating value, but also with new tensions that spring up from growing inequality. Against this background, Joseph Stiglitz, winner of the 2001 Nobel Prize in Economics, concluded that creating a *learning society* would be the biggest challenge for our future, a blueprint where the policies of learning are the building blocks for a democratic society (Stiglitz & Greenwald, 2014): "The most important 'endowment', from our perspective, is a society's learning capacities (which in turn is affected by the knowledge that it has; its knowledge about learning itself; and its knowledge about its own learning capacities)."

The role of universities in this new society must not be understated or trivialized; it must instead be scrupulously planned and pursued, connecting harmoniously with society and institutions.

Universities are the nerve centre in the "knowledge value chain", they play a part in creating new knowledge through their research and development, they transmit knowledge through pre- and post-degree teaching and play a key role in spreading knowledge in society.

It is not always easy to be the node connecting knowledge and society. The recent shock caused by the worldwide pandemic has thrown back to centre stage the debate on expertise and the role of scientific knowledge and its distinctive part in resolving complex problems. The absence of simple and unequivocal answers, typical of scientific method-based learning, together with the need to refer to objective and proven data before summing matters up, can be destabilizing when society is used to an overload of fast-paced news (and not necessarily true), and where opposing positions are too often based upon biased or preconceived opinions.

On the contrary, the landscape of education and developing knowledge is in constant evolution; new private subjects are assuming roles in domains that have traditionally been a prerogative of universities, research centres and large government laboratories. Space X has shown the world that great government agencies do not have exclusivity over space research, and Amazon and Google are setting the direction in many research fields, from logistics to artificial intelligence and self-drive vehicles, and are now dipping their toes into the waters of education.

In this landscape, universities are called upon to redefine their strategic place in society today and how it links to their original mission of developing and

---

36 Communication from the Commission, February 5, 2003 – The role of the universities in the Europe of knowledge.

transmitting *knowledge*. The scope of this subject is intricate and wide-reaching, meaning that we will concentrate in particular on four facets:

- the universities' level of focus in the areas of research and of teaching; in particular, on what do they base their preference for electing to be a specialist or generalist university, and when and how should they pursue a nucleation process or expand into new fields and disciplines
- level of inter-subject integration in teaching and research, identifying, in particular, the mechanisms and opportunities that can help or hinder cross-disciplinary teaching and research
- specialist or generalist research topics in which to invest; should they opt for research guided by the great global challenges and topics that make the most noise in scientific literature, or should they instead conduct scientific speculations into topics that have historically defined their own ecosystem, enabling them to consolidate their expertise in a given specialism
- impact over time and where the request for research originated, especially the built-in choices and level of harmony between research and innovation, between curiosity-driven and application-driven research, and between the various time scales of reference for the results of the research

If we analyse the polarities that can direct choices for each facet, technical universities, which historically have always been concerned with short- and medium-term transfer of knowledge, can set out future development paths that are more in tune with modern-day challenges and their context of reference.

4.1.1 The domains of knowledge: focused or broad

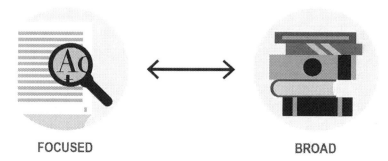

FOCUSED   BROAD

Technical universities have advanced along very similar historical lines; they were established at the request of their own economic and social fabric, and have played a fundamental role in the evolution of technical and scientific knowledge throughout different sets of circumstances and moments in time.

Today, many different elements are clamouring for their attention, requiring them to think hard and long about their place in the development of knowledge.

Firstly, the evermore rapid and pervasive evolution of technologies translates into the growing importance of their role in many fields of knowledge, whether in basic or in applied science. New computing technologies, new solutions that use artificial intelligence, new sensors, new production technologies, new materials and new integrated systems have become the enabling factors to produce new knowledge in many spheres. Nevertheless, the speed of technological change and the occasional unexpected negative impacts, both socially and environmentally, are compelling reasons to establish new harmony between the different knowledges, a melody between knowledge in the sciences and knowledge in the humanities. "Man" is recentred at the heart of knowledge development within a complex ecosystem that hinges on sustainability.

In addition, this landscape is the testing ground for global challenges, where the drive to extend the universities' operational spectrum to other spheres of knowledge is matched against the need to apply research models based on hard specialism and vertical knowledge, capable of braving complexity. If all these elements of change were projected to the future, they would probably be even faster and momentous; even so, there is an urgent need to reflect on the new role that technical universities can take on in their preferred spheres of knowledge.

The tension between focusing on a few thematic and disciplinary fields, on the one side, and disciplinary breadth on the other, affects several strategic options within a university, conditioning its choice of research to undertake, as well as the role it plays within its system of reference and in wider society.

Focusing enables universities to consolidate and steer their work to develop and transmit knowledge within a precise technical and disciplinary circle, with the objective of excelling in the national and international scene. Technical universities and business schools are highly focused entities created with the clear-cut mission to respond to the demand for research and the need for education that was expressed in a given context, against the backdrop of the Second and Third Industrial Revolutions, in a historical period of drive and propulsion. For this reason, focusing often means that a university must leverage on its own DNA, which is historically enrooted in a landscape intertwined with its own mission and thus a strong element in its identity, raising its potential as the preferred partner for specific topics. This particular strategy is a very effective way for a university to consolidate its connection to its local ecosystem, re-enforcing its impact on its urban surroundings and its local territory. A focused university can easily develop collaborative models based upon complementarity[37] in both teaching and research.

---

37 We can list many successful projects in medicine and engineering starting from the Harvard-MIT Program in Health Sciences and Technology (HST), one of the first interdisciplinary and inter-institutional educational programmes created in the 1970s (https://hst.mit.edu/about), up to the more recent projects like the Joint Georgia Tech & Emory University Biomedical Engineering PhD (https://bme.gatech.edu/bme/georgia-tech-emory-bme-phd-program), the recent project involving the University of Zurich (UZH), University of Basel, Università della Svizzera italiana (USI) and ETH on a new degree in medicine designed to increase the number of graduates in medicine in this area,

94 Strategic choices for universities of science and technology

When a university's areas of expertise are clear, it can choose the boundaries for its role within teaching and research collaborations with other institutions and actors and can access contiguous discipline fields or topics where there is the need for specific development work. By contrast, a focused university may find it difficult to create situations internally for cultural and scientific integration between separate fields or to move in cultural spheres other than those where it predominates. When faced with emerging fields and new frontiers, it must invest heavily and set in place very complex processes of integration to create the nucleus of the new subject area and then develop new thematic sectors internally.

The pros and cons are the exact mirror image for generalist universities, often historically enrooted within the pre-industrial revolution model of a university and where the processes of evolution have worked in favour of aggregating new disciplinary fields; today these universities offer a very wide spectrum of topics. However, the choice made in very focused universities to expand their range of subjects progressively is very much an ongoing trend, although the nuances vary to reflect specific identities and contexts of reference.

Compared to technical universities, the current convergence, especially between organic and inorganic sciences, and between engineering and sciences in biology and medicine, could indicate an opening to life sciences, a process that is already taking place in Europe's great technical and scientific universities. In this case, if we look at the complexity and multi-layered topics of reference, expanding the range of subjects by creating core fields internally could ensure better continuity and greater impact in both teaching and research, paving the way to internal actions that stimulate collaboration and thus respond to the challenges of complex problems.[38]

Furthermore, the increase in areas of scientific interest linked to emerging macro-phenomena, such as technological convergence, increases the universities' robustness and resilience, enabling them to meet variations in the demand for research from the outside world. On the downside, there would probably be the need for substantial investment to give universities the edge they need to be competitive in a field of institutions with an iron grip on the topics that are candidates for expansion, and in the long term, their identity could be weakened. It would, instead, be problematic for a technical university to expand its core subjects by nucleation to topics like social sciences and the humanities that are more distant, but which are becoming crucial in a system-wide overview of innovation. In

---

and the MEDTEC School programme between Politecnico di Milano and Humanitas. These projects are all similar, with different emphasis on education level (the Harvard-MIT programme covers master's and doctorates, Georgia Tech & Emory is only at PhD level, and the Zurich and Milan initiatives cover undergraduate and master's degrees) that stress the need to identify connecting paths between fields of knowledge in applied sciences (medicine and engineering in this case).

38 Over time, various technical universities have, bit by bit, brought in other fields of teaching and research, like the Technical University of Munich (TUM) which now features a School of Life Sciences, the Swiss Federal Institute of Technology Lausanne (EPFL) with its School of Life Sciences and College of Humanities, and Boston's Massachusetts Institute of Technology (MIT) which has a School of Humanities, Arts and Social Sciences and a School of Sciences.

technical and scientific universities, there is the risk that these disciplines could find the stage insufficiently rich or consolidated and be unable to spread their wings in teaching and research. They could potentially become the domain that services the other disciplines and thus without the depth of discipline-related knowledge necessary to take their proper place within their scientific community of reference.

The progress of knowledge is now increasingly connected to many different dimensions that combine disciplinary skills, in-depth explorations of new areas and cross-fertilization of domains. Technical universities must now identify the strategies for change and design their own model of evolution to promote and spur the development of new knowledge at the interface of disciplines. We can clearly see two viable models of change. One is a collaborative-relational model and the other a model of internal nucleation and growth, enacted through the creation of new schools, research centres and departments.

At this crossroad, many project variables come into play. A university must first identify the disciplines that need more urgent planning for internal development because they are intrinsically linked to processes of change that are investing the university's building block disciplines, its very DNA, and these need time and hefty resources. It must then identify disciplines that are necessary since they provide complementary knowledge and because of their role in the greater picture and their utility in view of collaborative arrangements. Alongside these processes, universities should implement strategies to connect with local actors and together plan long-term working relationships that factor in the needs that emerge from their industrial, economic and social ecosystems. Furthermore, they must seriously plan how to insert the new batch of subjects into the established processes of teaching and research. When technical universities can shape the inevitably long-term path of evolution for their spectrum of subjects, they will avoid finding themselves unready for the future requests of a society racing ahead at great speed.

4.1.2 Knowledge and its boundaries: disciplinarity or hybridization

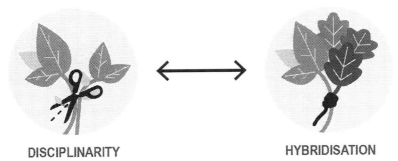

DISCIPLINARITY   HYBRIDISATION

The complexity of modern challenges and the need to respond to social and technological problems that are evermore convoluted and dynamic have required and still require a critical reflection on the forms and tools for creating and spreading knowledge. The universities' range of subjects and topics should be redefined and amplified, and subject boundaries redesigned, as must the models that encourage hybridization and dialogue among the various elements. The underlying reason is that it is now amply clear that innovation occurs in the space between different subjects, instigating new forms to develop and transmit knowledge in the novel ecosystem of "collaborative global research".

The tension between disciplinarity and integration must square up with an overhaul to all disciplinary-related parameters, assisted by new approaches to create and circulate knowledge that will open up domains of research and training at the boundaries between subjects. There is also the need to deal with the growing demand for subject depth and specialization, while subject specialization, in turn, particularly in domains with a strong technical and scientific element, is up against increasing technical intricacy and acceleration in the processes of technological change, all of which requires a good dose of specialism.

"Vertical" disciplinarity is often the most sound and direct route for designing and developing a clear-cut academic research profile, often set in relation to a particular scientific community or sector of reference. The development of new knowledge must be backed by a local community able to validate, assess and exploit the quality of results, through peer-to-peer reviewing. Universities that are strong in a particular set of subjects can establish their own distinctive identity and have a recognized presence within academic communities where the level of specialization is high, especially in technical and scientific settings. The recent health scare has put the spotlight on the importance and authority invested in serious degrees of specialism in these fields of knowledge. Furthermore, a strong vocation in a given subject has proven its worth by providing the basis of a subject, as it is much easier to anchor multi-disciplinary skills onto existing cognitive pillars and skills. Nevertheless, disciplinarity can lead to the fragmentation of knowledge, and sometimes excessive specialism can hinder rather than help the progress of knowledge (Russo, 2008). Exponential growth in available information and in topics of advanced research to be analysed is not always joined by processes whereby the information learnt is synthesized organically and the evolution of thought can be consolidated.

A path that instead inclines towards disciplinary integration within teaching and research is often less orthodox or accepted by the scientific communities of reference; it is also more difficult to design and support, because of the profusion of energy required to overcome all the barriers in communication erected by different cognitive models, languages and investigation tools, typical of every discipline. This kind of path often means a greater risk of failure and can have less impact in the short term, due to the inevitable difficulty of identifying a scientific community with the know-how to evaluate the output. In the medium to long term, there can be marked advances in knowledge, and even the discovery of new fields that surface through studies and investigations steeped in transdisciplinarity. A functional model will often come up with the answers to systemic problems that require all sorts of synthesizing operations, as is often the case in project challenges. In technical and scientific universities, developing a vocation for project experimentation that spans several disciplines can actually be the trigger for mechanisms of integration in both teaching and research, because it creates problem-oriented environments (teaching and research laboratories) instead of being centred on the subjects.

In pursuing policies that incentivize collaborations founded on solid disciplinary skills and strengthen collaborative approaches, a university's first objective must be a solid "ecosystem" of disciplinary skills flanked by laboratories and facilities for interdisciplinary and project-based research. The ensuing cross-fertilization between the various fields will arise through forms of dynamic aggregation involving researchers with complementary expertise, all in function of the same macro-objective. In this sense, local proximity can be a critical element to implement this creative potential throughout an entire system, deploying, among other tools, "commons", socialization structures and collaborative work.

It is, therefore, necessary to rethink the processes of creating knowledge, envisaging non-linear pathways in the careers and life-long learning of academic educators, which must be contemplated and guided. Freeing up their time to include study periods, including in subjects loosely connected or unconnected to their own research fields, is one possible method. We can imagine a future where life-long learning for researchers and teaching staff is nearly a must and can include horizontal studies. Sabbaticals could be "at home", giving researchers the freedom to expand their wealth of knowledge; engineers will study genetics or philosophy, architects can be absorbed in mathematics or data science, and biologists will learn about materials or robotics.

Today, at this moment of convergence between subjects and where the collective interest is turning to education and research focused on problems rather than on subjects, the choice between disciplinarity and integration seems a critical one. It is certainly particularly difficult for universities where there is an ongoing need to update and develop technical and scientific knowledge of escalating sophistication, but which are also under pressure to prefigure the impact of their work and test its applications in evermore transdisciplinary environments.

4.1.3 Knowledge development trajectories: identity or prominence

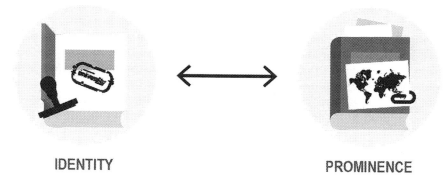

IDENTITY   PROMINENCE

Even the world of research is having to deal with the problems of globalization. Apart from the matter of attracting students and professors, where the promotional models are now very similar, there are also issues regarding research. The rapidity in publishing and divulging research results, as well as the general tendency to promote calls for funding geared towards solving the world's problems, are elements that drive investors to converge on and invest in high impact research topics with great potential, and these topics are often the same the world over. In contrast, the distinctive traits and specific factors of excellence of a university and its research groups, its history and its relationship with its reference ecosystem, in other words, its *identity*, can be a valuable hallmark when developing new knowledge. These two poles, global topics and excellent local institutes can provide the basis for strategic considerations on the *topics* of research.

The array of subject matter that constitutes a university's *research portfolio* is a strategic basic asset, capable of playing a fundamental part in the university's present and future positions on the relevant international stage. By research portfolio, we mean all the topics studied by the single research groups within a university.

In defining a portfolio, at one extreme is a model whose linchpin is *continuity* with the past and consolidation of positions achieved. In this case, the emerging profile is based upon *identity*, which is often enrooted in "schools" that have become established over the years. This knowledge development model is, in general, extremely stable and involves a vertical approach to individual subjects, with the university potentially achieving a dominant position in particular scientific and technological settings, and innovation is typically of an incremental kind. Universities will often focus on topics in response to requests from their own industrial and social ecosystem, and research groups tend to be on the same wavelength as their ecosystem. On the other hand, the main risk for a research system based on identity is its low level of mobility, and results are often based on incremental innovation that can, ultimately, lead to only marginally innovative outcomes. Sometimes the university can even find itself disconnected from its local social and economic fabric, being unable to keep up with the dynamics of new challenges emerging from its ecosystem.

At the other extreme, we can identify a "prominence-based" research system, where we have borrowed the term prominence from the bibliometric vocabulary to label emerging research topics that are "peaking", garnering a rise in interest from the international scientific community.

Obviously, being able to suss out the next prominent topics ahead of the scientific community of reference enables universities to exploit this model's potential, giving research groups a head start in driving the development of knowledge. *Super-research universities* will often choose this model; the topics of research are often extremely challenging and risky, but also of high potential and, if successful, open the way to totally unexplored avenues of research.

A more common situation is where the *prominence-based* model is adopted but tweaked, so that the university is a *follower*, without necessarily implying anything negative. Emerging research topics often have many facets, and there is room for everyone to contribute to new knowledge.

There are a number of factors that induce universities to opt for a *prominence-based* model. The list includes a globalized research market, rising competition among publishers that control the scientific publications market, and national mechanisms to evaluate research on the basis of the bibliometric impact of scientific publications. In addition, there is a proliferation of "top-down" financing schemes that steer the researchers' attention towards specific topics, often connected to global challenges contained in national and international frameworks.

Prominence-based research often means a better chance of accessing funds in competitive calls and improving the impact of one's scientific products. This model can also induce universities to switch research topics more often, so they never really develop the level of in-depth knowledge that makes them true "masters" in this area or gives them a clear and unique identity. In other words, interpreting the *prominence-based* model incorrectly can transform a group of researchers into a mere sounding board for keywords.

Clearly, the ideal way to solve this dichotomy is for several models to coexist within a research system. Virtuous and harmonious coexistence among research groups inspired by opposing paradigms of knowledge development could be a key element for success in a university projecting to the future.

However, rather than dwelling on the optimum mix of models, universities in 2040 will be expected to have an array of tools for their researchers to field during the *life-cycle of a research topic*, throughout the stages of conceiving new directions to explore, developing and consolidating knowledge in mature topics, and completing scientific speculations in topics where new challenges are unlikely.

The initial life cycle phase could be underpinned by *technology foresight* studies and centres, by doctorate programmes used as the testing ground for cutting-edge themes and promising yet challenging topics, as well as by recruiting young researchers in emerging fields and setting up workgroups and hubs that act as catalysts for researchers by cross-fertilizing knowledge. During the maturity stage, the results should be promoted and harnessed appropriately, and the research supported with adequate funds. In the final stage, the research group should be encouraged to scope out new challenges and further avenues of interest.

4.1.4 Applying and transferring knowledge: linearity or circularity

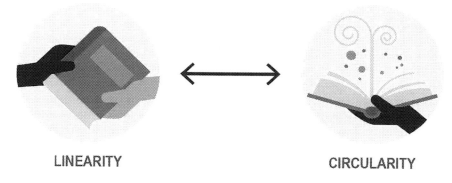

LINEARITY   CIRCULARITY

Today, the debate on the relationship between *basic* research, *applied* research and technological development is as hot as ever. Among the elements that come into play are the faster speed of generating knowledge and technologies in many fields, the many more public and private actors now involved in the processes of creativity and development, the urgency for companies to transform R&D into higher value added, and the surge in business competitivity. On top of this is the globalization of the research and innovation market and, above all, swelling competition to access public and private funding. Prompted by these factors, universities need to re-establish the balance between research elements that tend to be perceived as opposites, but which in reality should coexist in harmony. Equally, new forms of scientific research are emerging in response to progressively more complex problems arising from today's great social and technological challenges, establishing a new "collaborative global research" ecosystem, where the spreading and application of knowledge is bound up more and more closely with economic and social development.

As in all categorizations, that between basic research and applied research carries with it all the limits of oversimplification. The difficulty to classify complex and

Strategic choices for universities of science and technology **101**

diverse processes, like those linked to the creation of new knowledge, emerges in the terminology, which struggles to be shared or be unequivocal[39]

The synonyms abound for basic research alone, with terms like *fundamental research, early research, background research, long-term research,* progressing to *curiosity-driven, blue-sky science, bottom-up* and so on.

To try and explore this polarity, we must start from the logic underpinning the distinction. First, we must review the idea that knowledge is created in a *linear process* where the basic research results are the starting point for applied research, and the successive stages are when these results are developed, diffused and utilized in business and society. This model is found in the sociology of science, where, in talking about the process of creating scientific knowledge, *Mode 1* is when the only purpose is to advance knowledge without there being an immediate application for the results, and *Mode 2* is where multi-disciplinary teams work in a defined period of time on problems motivated by a precise application (Gibbons et al., 1994).

The second element underpinning the polarity between basic science and applied science is historically connected to the mechanisms of funding research. One facet applies to the programmes (and budgets) for "basic research" (Pillar 1 in European framework programmes and the funding opportunities offered through the US National Science Foundation federal agency). The other facet is for "applied research" (Pillar 2 in European programmes and the funding awarded by government departments in the United States). Increasingly often, the calls for funding proposals include references to Technology Readiness Levels (TRLs). TRLs relate to the advancement of technical maturity of the topic at hand and are an important measure of project progress.

Although research funding tends to keep the various fields and encourage polarization, we must not take it for granted that a university's strategy should be to replicate this distinction internally. Narayanamurt and Odumosu (2016) state that demolishing the barriers between basic and applied sciences is the right route to sustain and propel future advancement of knowledge.

Many examples in the history of science show that the development of new knowledge is, in reality, a decisively non-linear process, with continuous cycles switching between innovation and research, as in the case of information technology (Figure 4.2), or in the defence of "the usefulness of useless knowledge", as set out by Abraham Flexner, the founding Director of the Institute for Advanced Study at Princeton (Flexner, 2017).[40] The future development of knowledge will

---

39 "No category of sciences exists to which one could give the name of applied sciences. There are science and the applications of science, linked together as fruit is to the tree that has borne it." – Louis Pasteur

40 Flexner shows many representative examples to emphasize the needs of research not specifically driven by targeted objectives. As is the case of Paul Ehrlich, a leading figure in both modern antibiotic research and drug discovery, inventor of the first therapy to treat syphilis and Noel prize winner in Medicine. One day Wilhelm von Waldeyer, Paul Ehrlich's supervisor, asked his student what he was working on, as he was so busy tinkering aimlessly with bacterial broths and Petri dishes. Ehrlich simply replied "Ich probiere" – "I am just fooling around."

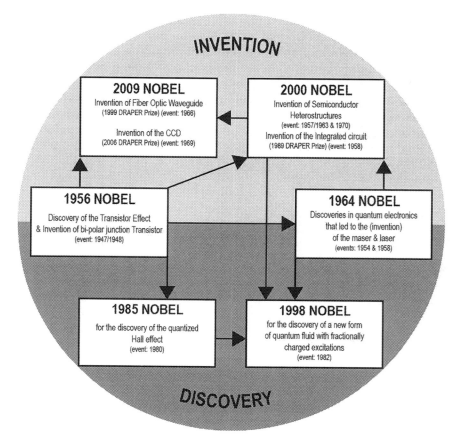

FIGURE 4.2 Invention & discovery cycle: all major advancements in information technology are based on the many exchanges between undertakings in basic research and in technological innovation.

be played out through new models that bridge disciplines and get research at different TRL levels to talk to each other, as set out in "Pasteur's Quadrant" (Figure 4.3), which contains research representing great progress in knowledge and of immediate application in society.

Facing a demand for knowledge that evolves faster than ever before, the traditional model that expects research results to be translated into applied research, and ultimately into a technological transfer, is incompatible or ineffective. The risk in this model is to build barriers and dig holes in the transfer of knowledge, which can lead to "death valleys" for scientific and technological progress in society.

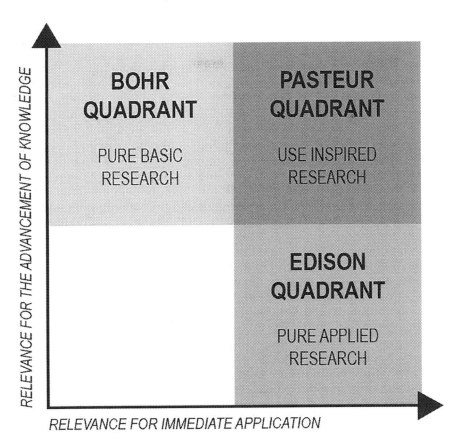

FIGURE 4.3   Pasteur's quadrant (Donald Stokes).

We must promote projects for research and innovation that embrace research demands which vary in terms of impact, at high or low TRL levels (market-driven or closer to basic research), with multi-disciplinary teams that cover discipline spectra with very different premises.

As a consequence, we must redesign research doctorates as the thread linking research studies along different timelines, establishing teams that work on linked topics with different outlooks which can connect basic science to applied science.

4.2 Relationships – actors interacting in the university system

The future of technical universities will be decided by their relative degree of openness or closure, especially towards their peers but also towards other actors, with regard to teaching, research, the capacity to innovate, relationships with educational systems in single countries and at the international level.

104 Strategic choices for universities of science and technology

These two ideal types are, on the one side, a self-sufficient and self-contained university that excels in research and features high-profile researchers who are unique in their field, and which produces all its teaching material on its own and aspires to educate a national or global elite. On the other side is the more open, network-connected university that comes up with good research because of its meticulous infrastructure and extended research groups. This second university networks with other universities in its teaching offer, which belongs to the solid nation- or continent-wide university systems of good average quality that addresses a potentially broad audience of young people aspiring to receive a technical education.

Naturally, no university fits perfectly into one of the two models; while sharing and projecting towards the outside has been the blueprint of universities since the Middle Ages, it is certainly true that they also feature a strong internal organization. The intensity and density of their relationships and internal connections is a major trait, as is a faculty that identifies with its university, especially when in competition for dwindling resources.

At the same time, we believe that this polarization is effective, as it gives an intuitive and immediate representation of the two models between which universities are swaying and have always swayed.

We will try and set out a few apparently opposing pairings and use them to hypothesize several directions of evolution that are in the sights of, or the ground is being prepared by, technical universities that wish to project themselves to the future.

- The polarity between self-sufficiency and collaboration in a network approach is addressed both from the teaching side, where it partially intersects professor and student mobility, and from the research side, where it intersects with sources of investment and infrastructure.
- Research relationships are examined from the opposing corners of research stars and tightly knit research teams, where factors linked to the recruitment of teaching and research faculty become particularly important.
- The different forms of "doing" teaching, from interacting physically with students to interacting via digital tools, is a question that can play out along several dimensions, starting from classes that are totally in presence and live, to a range of alternatives that deploy asynchronous and mixed models and are based on active learning, alongside more passive traditional methods.
- In a university's relationship with its students, the crossroad for teaching relates to the pros and cons of standardized or personalized teaching paths, to give students a wider perspective and more choice.
- Finally, the classical contrast between universities for the masses or for the elite (of selected students) is re-interpreted from a broader viewpoint that looks into the scale of education systems in single countries, and the education system in continental Europe overall, framed against other parts of the world.

4.2.1 The provision of education: self-standing or sharing

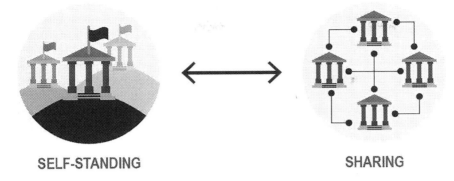

SELF-STANDING   SHARING

🔍

The university system has nearly always been international, and certainly from before globalization. Knowledge is spread through the flow of students, first by carrying young people in from the developing world to the capitals of more advanced countries, then seeking them out as a tool of cultural hegemony and, finally, by creating a true market where universities compete globally to attract students (Varghese, 2008). The most recent trends highlight a highly polarized international system, with increasing inter-university competition to tempt the best students from around the world. While the dominant logic in the United States is still encapsulated in the "excel to compete" model and every university is concerned with its own subjective strategy, universities in Europe have been questioning themselves for some time about how to implement a different vision, one that can be summed up in the paradigm of "excel to cooperate". This model intends to build a solid platform of collaboration between universities, within countries and across Europe but will have to overcome the hurdle of universities often perceiving themselves as being in competition. The idea could nevertheless be a plausible answer to empower the European knowledge space amid the dynamics afoot in the rest of the world.

This different approach for Europe is the upshot of the many traditions and differences in teaching, organization and research that have induced the European Union to use university cooperation as a powerful tool for cultural integration and create a new generation that is more linked to the spirit of unity than to national states (Mitchell, 2012). The clearest example is the student exchange programme Erasmus, in one or other of its incarnations, and there are other collaboration programmes funded through the European Commission, such as the recent "European Universities Initiatives".

Another element of differentiation relates to the outstanding positions in various fields of knowledge, which, in systems like those in place in the United States, tend to concentrate in a few universities that outperform in nearly every area, while in

Europe they are scattered across a wider group of universities, each excelling in a few areas (Bonaccorsi et al., 2017). Although this diversity may have originated from different practices to recruit teaching faculty (the one very much based on autonomy and the other closely bonded to national laws), it is certainly pushing Europe towards complementarity-based cooperation.

Within this general trend, it is still possible to conceive policies geared towards excellence in technical universities. In 20 years or so, the timeline examined in this document, these policies in the sphere of teaching could push either for a predominant model of self-sufficiency and isolated competition or for cooperation enacted through academic networks of excellence.

In the sphere of teaching, the advantages of an independent and self-sufficient model stand out clearly when we analyse the need for coherence and order in curricula that can cater for a wide body of students, with all their different educational backgrounds and levels, pointing them towards sound technical and scientific skills that can be easily pitched on the job market. In Europe, the tradition of technical universities rolling out very structured degree programmes that produce a highly qualified workforce with strong project-based skills is a distinctive part of the European industry. There has always been competition between universities in every European country to turn out graduates of a high standard vied for by employers and, with greater pan-European mobility, it has become a continental situation. Furthermore, this model allows the enactment of worthwhile policies to connect the local area and reference ecosystem to, for example, the professional profiles in demand.

This traditional approach is now being put under discussion by the speed at which professions are changing, themselves the outcome of the increased pace of technological and scientific progress. The flexibility and capacity of adaption required of new professionals do not mix well with rigid programmes. The confirmation comes from employers, who are expressing their appreciation of more varied courses that include periods abroad and cross-fertilization between subjects.

Strategic partnership networks, like IDEA League and Alliance4Tech, are clearly pointing the way for certain institutions (those in a position to ensure excellent standards in their specialist fields of education and research) to cooperate in a Europe-wide bubble of teaching and research. Universities could build an international environment open to diversity and welcome the best students and professors from within the partnership as a whole. Under such an umbrella scheme, students and researchers could spend periods in the best universities and institutions in Europe and globally (even outside the university world), advancing the process of internationalization that had started with Erasmus through more rigorously structured programmes. In general, the consolidation of a network model allows universities to retain control over the careers of their students, who otherwise would be likely to build their study programmes elsewhere in this closely interconnected world, potentially turning to universities beyond their domestic shores, as is already somewhat the case.

As a final corollary, universities could concentrate their offer more directly on the set of vocational lines where they excel in a logic of mutual complementarity with research and academic courses offered by their partners; looking forward, the partnership could even be expanded to online learning aggregators. To achieve this purpose, the network must be designed very precisely, picking out the most suitable partners and sharing development strategies.

This level of cooperation is obviously not simple to achieve, and translating this vision into concrete programmes has already exposed several difficulties. Naturally, there are issues linked to the selection of the most fitting partners and to aligning everyone's objectives as well as the organizational structures underpinning the academic part. Another aspect not to be overlooked is that every university will need to retain a certain level of visibility over its own brand and take credit for its own outstanding results.

The balance in teaching between independent competition and network cooperation will depend upon the specific features of each university, those of the country and area where it is located, and the requirements of the various stakeholders, starting from those of the job market. Current university networks could evolve into a sort of "clubs of excellence", where students move fairly freely within small groups of selected universities and build their own study programmes from a pool of wide-ranging and diverse curricula. These "clubs" could compete independently in Europe and, acting as a single entity, rival other *super-research universities* across the world, attracting students interested in being educated within a setting with the undeniable strengths of flexibility and personalization.

4.2.2 *Working in research: competition or collaboration*

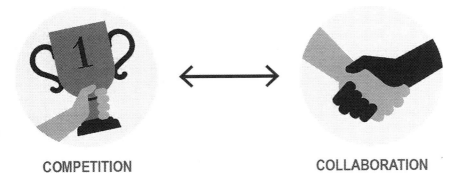

🔍

If we examine the system in its entirety, the research approaches and modalities in the various research centres are influenced by a complex set of factors, including the very significant role played by public demand in countries where universities are predominantly public, as well as in those with a significant section of private universities. Public sector demand could be directed more or less intensely towards basic or applied research (one only needs to think about the weight of defence-related work).

In Europe especially, the European Commission's framework programmes have, for some time, been driving applied research (both industrial and pre-competitive), steering the direction and perspective of research, especially in countries like Italy where national funding is more modest. Another model, taken up by the National Science Foundation in the United States and the European Research Council, provides funding to basic research, including the curiosity-driven and bottom-up type. The weight of research financed by the public purse (by regions, countries or supranationally) and the predominant direction of the demand for research can together generate different *research-scapes*, within which individual universities can set their own strategies. In general, calls for applied research require building broad transnational consortia and so spur the search for partnerships, as clearly shown in many EU framework programmes. Collaboration thus becomes both the programme's means and its end.

Within this panorama, universities can move between two poles, either attempting to achieve excellence on an individual plane, or positioning themselves within solid formal research networks that bring together other universities on the domestic and, more importantly, international stage.

There are natural flows of arguments for and against either option. *Super-competitive* universities, those geared towards individual excellence (the best-known being a handful of private US universities and a few British ones with their enduring heritage), are able to set the course for the trends and visibility of future research topics through the choices they make, because of the reputation they wield. Because of their status, these universities and their researchers are always the first to explore new frontiers, and never have to hook themselves up to the efforts of others, giving them a clear competitive edge. At the same time, it is difficult to always be trailblazers, in part because of the work to source funding for not-yet consolidated research lines by relying on the university's or research centre's reputation alone. In addition, being at the coalface of innovation in many different fields and disciplines can be burdensome, as investing primarily in some fields can lead to less fertile research in others. Unless a university/team is closely bound into a network of its peers, this effort must be concentrated within every single structure.

Working within consolidated research networks can have many benefits. Firstly, the complementarity among different subjects can be fully exploited, as each university can deploy its own points of excellence within every single research area or topic, linking its own strengths up with those of others without having to oversee discontinuity and the frontiers of innovation in every field. Solid network connections can additionally encourage the establishment of interdisciplinary research groups because it is easier to test out forms of constructive dialogue within networks where many nodes are, in essence, equivalent. The territorial scale for networks to be effective, and make sense from the perspective of advancing research, can vary substantially. In cases where universities share physical facilities and laboratories, for example, networks will be dense and institutions generally close to each other geographically. Other times, the relationship can imply much "longer" networks, potentially even with global reach.

Operating constructively and continuously through networks can raise problems. Maintaining an alignment of objectives between subjects with dissimilar features becomes more difficult as time goes by. Universities that differ in their history, vocation and location (within regional or national contexts) can evolve at different rates, and their objectives may not correspond to the objectives more generally within their networks. Furthermore, when networks are cohesive and robust, the contribution made by single research teams or universities may fall under the radar, which is an obvious risk should they want to go it alone in certain programmes or projects as, differently from the super-competitive universities, the reputation of individual institutions in a network may not be sufficiently well established.

Overall, building and consolidating research areas and topics should be read in a dynamic perspective, in view of giving every university the option to intervene rapidly in promising areas, while always utilizing the contribution of the others. Areas that may be supervised less in one phase must not be allowed to dry up excessively and so cannot be made fertile and active when they are needed (e.g. that topic is once again included in research policy agendas).

Finally, for analytical clarity, we have examined as separate items the benefits and disadvantages for universities to run their teaching and research within a network. It is, however, important to read the two aspects together. Given that networks are contingent on relationships between people engaged in teaching and research (especially teaching faculty, PhD students and young researchers), dealing with the two aspects together is positive for the quality, depth and soundness of inter-university sharing. Teaching, for instance, can certainly benefit from the content and experimentation of shared research.

4.2.3 Research actors: stars or teams

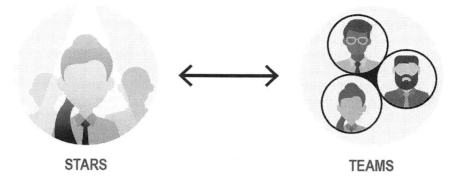

STARS   TEAMS

The dilemma between consolidated research networks, on the one side, and universities striving for individual excellence, on the other, is mirrored on a smaller scale within the universities themselves. They will often be torn between building and supporting laboratory facilities and internal research networks that are more horizontal in scope, and attracting great figureheads, researchers pounding the international stages of excellence whose personal reputations are outstanding. Recruiting personnel in the high-intensity university workplace is critical for the university's development.[41] Country by country, the institutional regulations and arrangements concerning tertiary education play a fundamental role in determining the levels of freedom, and thus the autonomy of individual universities, in making decisions about their staff. We can roughly identify two broad models. One involves a more standardized and regulated recruitment process (including competitive procedures) and the other relates to processes involving negotiations between the university and individual researchers. In countries like France, Italy and Spain, the recruitment process is more standardized than in Germany, Switzerland and the United Kingdom.

Another significant variable, looking at career pathways, is linked to whether the prevalent pattern is for academics to pursue their careers within a single university or whether they are more open to frequent transfers that mark the stages of their career. This facet is also influenced by institutional and cultural variables, but each university has several levers to steer the path of their young researchers in one direction or another.

---

41 OECD (2019), "Benchmarking higher education system performance", in *Higher Education*, OECD Publishing, Paris.

In this setting, the universities' first path may be to recruit, where possible, individual standout researchers, whenever it is felt that they can bring to the table a high reputation and be a strong factor in acquiring substantial funding.

This strategy can be very effective when universities are able to identify researchers of excellence in the early stages of their careers and attract them by creating ad hoc research units or laboratories that will allow the academics to make a jump in quality, along with raising the profile of their universities. Structures created to attract the single brilliant researcher tend to be pyramids that function hierarchically, although the context will determine differences. In some countries, such as the United States, the outstanding researcher is likely to work with a group of PhD students and post-docs; elsewhere, as in several European countries, they will work within a more diverse team of people at different stages in their careers.

The general risk is that research stars have very dynamic careers and can move around quite frequently drawn by attractive offers from competing universities, thus weakening the universities that had invested highly in them at one point or another in their careers.

Universities could instead build more horizontal research structures, based on networks of researchers and laboratories, potentially creating more durable arrangements. This model is the opposite of the proceeding one, and often involves research networks and groups that become established over time, frequently through internal career paths, with skills being shared and broader groupings of disciplines. To some extent, this approach connects to the enduring concept of "school" as both a collective and a cohesive entity grouped around research topics and traditions.

The disadvantages compared to the option of employing researchers with a star cachet are much lower visibility and lesser impact of individual researchers, who are thus less able to endorse the attractiveness of resources. The other facet of this model is the obvious benefits of researchers identifying with their team (and university), more opportunities for them to work together, and their cumulative resilience if one of their numbers moves away.

As we have seen single universities are unlikely to control all the levers when they opt for one or the other model because much will depend on their connections with the supervisory system and with higher governing strata. However, as far as they can exert their autonomy, it is crucial that universities should know which selection criteria to implement regarding the various discipline fields, the evolution of research topics internationally and the need for infrastructure consequent of these choices.

4.2.4 Relationship between professors and students: digital or physical

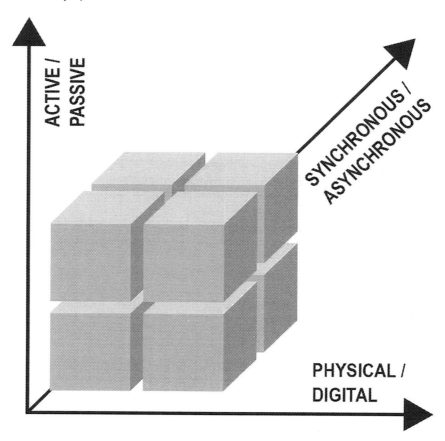

In recent years and especially latterly in our Covid-19 life, digital and connectivity tools have overturned the people-information relationship, as well as our social interaction, in ways and with ramifications that have been amply discussed on many occasions. It is however a fact that, before we were blown away by the health pandemic in spring 2020, these changes only brushed lightly against the university world, and even the technical and scientific universities had continued in their somewhat traditional ways of teaching and organizing their work. They had apparently sidestepped online learning, or e-learning, which had entered their lives years ago in specific domains, mainly those linked to professional training and education for companies.

We need to make an exception for massive open online courses (MOOCs), which have evolved at a supersonic rate, initially attracting great media interest

Strategic choices for universities of science and technology **113**

with high expectations for the democratization of university education. MOOCs were next seen as an opportunity for cultural and professional growth, principally for people with jobs and academic qualifications (Selingo, 2014), and finally have moved on to the current vision that tends to see them as a way of innovating teaching and as an active classroom management tool (Fassbinder et al., 2015). From a certain angle, the rapid evolution of the MOOC "hyper-cycle" has affected and, in part, restricted the full range of digital tools enabled by today's technology from being adopted, and only recently has there been a return to more considered planning.

The defining element of the current stage is to rethink teaching techniques to introduce, albeit slowly, active learning methodologies, where students no longer listen passively to lessons imparted by professors (the traditional *lectio* model). Instead, they are engaged individually or in groups, and directly involved in the process of expounding and absorbing knowledge (*active learning*), where sessions can be preceded by personal study, with material accessed from a number of sources, including online, and succeeded by sessions involving debate and guided problem-solving (*flipped classrooms – Sancassani 2019*).

It is interesting to note that this evolution in the world of education runs in parallel with that in the workplace, with the introduction of concepts like *smart working*, giving staff flexibility and independence about when and where they work, along with greater responsibility for objectives and results, and *agile-working*, which adds flexibility to the management of teams working on projects, so people and skills can be slotted in and out when needed, without the rigid boundaries of traditional organizational hierarchies. Interactive digital tools clearly have a critical role to play here also. Within the organization of universities, there has always been a distinction between work practices for teaching staff and those for administrative staff, with broad margins of flexibility for the teaching body (at least in their research work) and often rather traditional models for staff in administration.

It is plain that the global crises engendered by Covid-19 has rapidly upturned this picture and could potentially cause the pace of change to accelerate, having forced nearly all universities to try out distance learning methods and use a wide range of digital tools, and has driven all organizations towards smart-working, including in academia. The way teaching and work in universities is organized in a post-Covid-19 world will inevitably draw from the enforced experience of using digital tools and interacting remotely, and could lead to a total review of all the networks of contacts and interactions that normally underpin university life in time and space. Networks could be expanded to take in inter-university cooperation and, helped by the digital technology, could overcome, at least in part, the constraints of distance and the complexity of organizing student and professor mobility.

The potential choices of how to sort out teaching and work in tomorrow's technical universities throw up several polarities. Here we will focus on the relationship between *physical interaction and interaction mediated through digital tools*, on *interacting actively or passively* in learning and work practices, and on *synchronous or asynchronous involvement*.

Without question, university traditions everywhere in the world are built on a learning model that espouses the value of teaching in presence. A university student's path is, and in the future will remain, much more than a mere sequence of skills learnt. It is a path of personal growth based on student life and social interaction, assembling a wealth of experiences, endeavours, mistakes in projects and laboratory work, connecting with professors and researchers out of class, and building a network of relations that young people carry forward in their professional life. For students, their time at university means being immersed in a broth of opportunities for cultural and personal growth, adding to it creativity and a sense of initiative, and absorbing from it basic skills that reflect their personal characters and interests.

In the case of technical and scientific universities, a further ingredient is the experiential side, learnt through practical laboratory work and projects undertaken alone or in teams. The physical spaces of learning, with their equipment and facilities, are possibly the strongest endorsement of the importance of a university campus as the tangible place where students construct their studies and their path.

University campuses play a fundamental role as cultural centres for the entire local population in the cities and regions where they are located, enlivening public debate and giving non-experts the chance to approach specialist topics. The tens of thousands of students physically on the spot define the identity of many university cities and are often major contributors to the local economy.

It is clear that there is the reverse side of the coin in the physical presence of a university, linked to the high costs of building and maintaining the facilities, the daily commute of thousands of people from the surrounding areas, the non-minor environmental impact of all the activity and movement, and the difficulties of living among lots of people squashed into a small area.

With the advances in technology, evermore sophisticated and user-friendly digital tools offer new opportunities for accessing information and social interaction that can, at least in part, replace in-presence teaching. Obviously, digital applications can not only displace some forms of physical interaction but also introduce a rather radical change in the way integrations are structured and organized. In teaching, we are forced to rethink how we create the material we offer students (videos and online content in general) and the timings for managing teaching (like the flipped classroom). In providing services, all "over the counter" type services will be transformed. In work practices, teaching faculty and technical and administrative staff alike will connect and interact according to new sets of modalities, and the sharing and planning of tasks and objectives will also be different.

The most visible element of change is probably linked to time management in the lives of all the people orbiting around a university, and the consequences may not always be positive in the uneasy separation and overlap between teaching and/or work and personal life.

Strategic choices for universities of science and technology   **115**

The second dimension is often intertwined with the physical/digital dimension and is linked to the distinction between active interaction and elaborating information passively or accomplishing tasks autonomously.

In teaching, active or passive learning is a particularly topical issue. In standard university programmes, there is the tendency to prefer passive learning, and programmes and processes are occasionally on a repeat loop. Recent pedagogical trends underline the importance of active learning as the means to absorb and elaborate knowledge more efficiently. Study programmes can be personalized and students can learn how to be flexible in their learning, a skill that will be useful throughout their professional life when having to deal with fast-paced change. If we put the spotlight on the merits of the learning required in technical and scientific universities, often defined by the theoretical and methodological complexity of the matter covered, we can deduce that it is important to balance active and passive learning. The effort of abstraction, so much the part of modern science, entails the need for individual periods of listening/reading and absorbing the theoretical basic architecture, as well as the need for experiential sessions, bringing into play the methodological tools best suited to professor-student and peer-to-peer interaction.

Active and passive interaction also extends to on-campus work, at least partially, and applies to both research and services, where there is a combination of teamwork, collaborations and occasions/necessity for people to work autonomously.

The third dimension is linked to both the physical/digital and active/passive dimensions and relates to the element of time in person-to-person interaction and access to information, which can be synchronous or asynchronous.

Within the teaching world, possibly because MOOCs have distorted perceptions in the recent past, digital tools are often associated with a learning environment where the material is accessed asynchronously, and the actual learning process is at the time and place of one's choosing. The many universities that turned to distance learning as a consequence of Covid-19 discovered that digital tools designed for smart-working (such as video conferencing) are equally effective in teaching.

The general preference for synchronous dynamics is often linked to the interwoven spheres of learning and social interaction, invariably impossible to disentangle and often typical of the world revolving around a university campus. Digital tools can help to mix synchronous and asynchronous interaction in novel ways, and time can be managed more efficiently.

A simple example can help to explain this point, showing how one university tradition has evolved in step with the instruments available. Study groups are a very common form of social interaction among students. The group dynamic can transit from being mostly synchronous, where students study and discuss the various subjects together, to mixed modalities, where people still study together but independently, and raise questions or open discussions later, or whenever they arise, in unprogrammed asynchronous sessions. Digital tools enable synchronous and asynchronous interactions in the presence, and at a distance, and are an easy way to share material and information. Nevertheless, we must not remove the social and development value of people within a group meeting face to face in the social spaces of a university campus. Things work very similarly in research groups and among people responsible for university services.

In conclusion, we can certainly state that digital tools will change interactions within the university world at their very core. However, they can also be seen as an expansion to the teaching and social toolkit, where the opportunities to plan academic paths and methods of collaboration can be extended significantly. The norm in the future will probably be a mix of physical and digital working practices, with tools in keeping with who uses them (professors and students, students and students, research teams, university services staff) and for what reason. Networks for international collaboration will use digital technology to knock down the barriers of physical distance. Digital tools will ensure that teaching spaces become even more permeable to external input from industry.

4.2.5 Different learning pathways: uniformity or customization

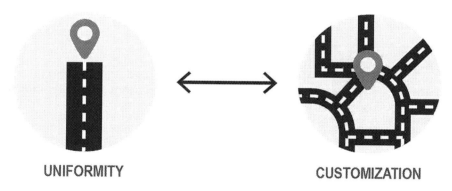

In a world where tertiary education has become universal, the students' motivation is a central factor for efficient education and learning, alongside their capacity to play an active role in the training process. This objective is often pursued in teaching processes by actively involving students and using multimedia and interactive teaching methods. An excellent method to spur motivation, but which is regularly somewhat overlooked, is to personalize the students' study programmes so as to develop their individual interests and inclinations. The teaching model adopted in the wake of the Bologna process severely curtailed the element of personalization, as it standardized programmes, confining students to a particularly passive role within their own study paths. The same is true for teaching faculty, who are generally incentivized with blanket mechanisms of productivity, while the option of personalizing their professional growth could drive the professors' motivation and increase results. Let us look at how we can break down the choice between a model that encourages personalized paths and one that retains a high level of standardization.

Standardized paths have the undeniable benefit of ensuring that students on exit have a solid preparation grounded in well-tested material and skills validated throughout enduring relationships with the local productive fabric, relationships which, in the case of technical and scientific universities, are both intense and constructive.

This approach is certainly the method prescribed in quality assurance models recently set up in many countries, especially in public universities. In these times of declining resources, public control over university education and professor recruitment is a way to ensure that funds are spent wisely and planned education programmes are validated through tools attesting that skills learnt will be of immediate practical use in the workplace. As we have already mentioned, this model is also closest to the European tradition of technical and scientific universities that act as guarantors in their local economy, meaning that businesses know that they can safely recruit an army of graduates as their workforce because, while their characteristics may be very similar, they are solid and easily utilized. Having standard parameters for recruiting and promoting faculty means that the quality in the teaching body is uniform throughout.

The future perspective seems to be a world dominated by the technological lever, where technical and scientific knowledge is becoming increasingly more important than social and economic sciences when educating the executive class. If we want technical and scientific universities to be involved in training an executive class that can govern the processes of change, they need study programmes that do not continuously retrace the common route, at least for a subgroup of students.

Several possible directions emerge from observing models that offer greater personalization while avoiding the trap of rewarding opportunistic behaviour (students taking the easiest options). On one side is the *mentorship* model, where mentoring is seen as an essential part of the professors' set of tasks, as they could guide small groups of students in their programme choices, even drawing on resources from outside the single university, as per the network model. On the other is the *meritocratic autonomy* model, which means rewarding students with greater freedom of choice proportionally to their results.

Both models contain an element of risk with personalization, which implies exploring untested paths and educational results that are not totally predictable. When students have a mentor to guide them, the risks are lessened, because the students' desire to try out new things meets the mentor's experience in identifying the right opportunities and mindset. Meritocratic autonomy gives more exploring space to people who have the mental ability to extract the best from any experience and avoid pitfalls or incoherencies in their training. Both mentorship and meritocratic autonomy require a substantial concentration of cognitive and strategic resources. Adopting one or other should be based on a careful analysis of the various personalization requirements that originate from particularly promising individual characteristics or from the need to explore new professional profiles that have yet to be consolidated.

In both cases, tapping into networks of strategic partnerships is a particularly intriguing approach, as students can construct their own individual learning pathways from a range of educational offers within a network of complementary universities.

Professors could take career paths defined by their own interests and potential. As is already the case in some countries, this possibility would outline careers geared more towards research or teaching, or even business. Going along these lines would place greater emphasis on individual skills, and so increase productivity within the university. This direction inevitably implies differentiated mechanisms of evaluation, as well as weighing up the risk of creating "first tier" and "second tier" paths.

As we have seen, organizational models in teaching must be redesigned if the chosen route is to personalize paths within a wider educational offer consisting, for example, of small standard modules that can be put together in a flexible way, to accommodate personal interests as well as the profiles and skills demanded by the job market. In addition, universities must take on the mantle of reliable and ongoing guides to help every student design a path in line with their abilities and ambition, which also matches up with the potential openings, jobs and their role in society. In a similar way, the inevitable personalization of academic paths for the teaching body will require a cultural and organizational shift for the universities going down this route.

4.2.6 The purpose of education: rights or merits

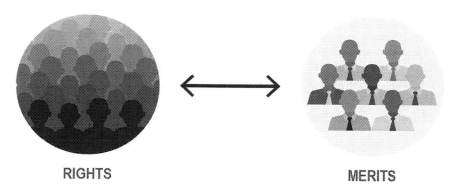

The systems of tertiary education vary from country to country, even within regions that are relatively homogeneous from a social and economic perspective. In particular, looking at Europe and the United States, the main difference is between countries with a high average quality of infrastructure (Sweden is an excellent example) and countries where there are some outstanding world-class universities, a high number of average ones and many that basically serve the educational needs of their local community (the United States is often cited in this context).[42] In general, simplifying rather, we can say that the standards of quality are very uniform throughout the systems in continental and Mediterranean Europe (so excluding the United Kingdom), while the opposite is true in the United States and, up to a point, China.

This traditional arrangement has been reshuffled over the past 30 years or so through reforms to the various university systems, which have introduced a model of autonomy based on control at a distance, with some local differences. According to this approach, which is derived from *new public management* in English-speaking countries, universities are given greater freedom, for example, in allocating their budgets, counterbalanced by subsequent checks and controls on the part of the state. The outcome of this model, combined with the fact that public resources for universities overall are now much scarcer, has been to trigger a wave of competition among universities nationally and internationally, and it has driven a large number of them to chase as many qualifications and accreditations as possible (Aghion et al., 2010), especially in some areas and fields (see Section 4.2.2).

Faced with these trends, technical universities in Europe have come up to a fork in the road. They could decide to remain universities for the masses, inserted within a relatively uniform national and pan-continental network of tertiary education, providing good university instruction to scores of young people. They could, otherwise, opt to ready themselves for an audience of highly selected students, probably reducing their overall numbers (while securing solid sources of alternative funding from research contracts or other forms of financing) and becoming universities for the elite.

Even if the processes of selective admission have always been based on merit, there is an inevitable link with the issue of social equality, because selection processes will struggle to assess the potential of students at the start of their university studies and tend to amplify pre-existing differences.

Apart from the weight of *path dependency* (the fact that traditionally most European technical universities are universities for the masses), there are strong arguments in favour of retaining such status. These universities address the serious need to

---

42 OECD (2019), *Education at a glance 2019: OECD indicators*, OECD Publishing, Paris. Fondazione Res (2016), *Università in declino. Un'indagine sugli atenei da Nord a Sud*, edited by Gianfranco Viesti, Donzelli, Rome.

educate the new classes of professionals in societies where knowledge and technological progress are increasingly taking centre stage, by imparting a solid technical and scientific skillset, well-developed critical strength to manage and use innovative technological solutions, and new problem-setting and problem-solving abilities.

To respond to these needs, and to the inevitably more standardized education that universities for the masses are able to offer, taking the current European two-level model (bachelor's and master's) as the starting point, there is the obvious problem of designing something that works at both levels. The first level must include basic material, although it should also have a certain professional content for students who do not intend to continue beyond this level. Added to this there is the more general question of identifying and selecting the most talented and deserving students throughout the entire process (from undergraduate studies to master's levels and then to doctorates).

In turn, the model of a highly selective university is interesting under certain aspects, if we imagine that national university systems will evolve towards models that are differentiated internally and more specialized. An elite university may be able to propose experimental paths that are focused and moulded to the individual student and where there is a close connection between research and innovation. Students could be selected very carefully, to create classrooms of brilliant students who can be involved in a range of different educational ventures (see Section 4.2.4), prioritizing forms of active learning.

In addition, a technical university for the elite can help to create a technically knowledgeable executive class. In today's complex societies, it is important that those who guide the country and society, and take on the responsibility of making major decisions, should master the main elements of technological innovation and know how to read them critically within the context of more general social and economic development, with all their ensuing ethical and political implications.

The main problem of universities for the elite is the very real risk of, in practice, selecting and admitting students not so much on the basis of their talent and individual ability, but because of family privilege. The OECD analysis has shown that, in many countries and increasingly frequently, people's individual careers reflect the social and economic status of their families of origin, and this is becoming very apparent in some countries (Agasisti et al., 2018). There is a high likelihood of mainly selecting students with a family background that was advantageous to them in their school years. The obvious problems with equality (since access to schools of excellence should be based on personal ability not on family) are compounded by issues relating to effective development, because social mobility would come to a standstill, with evident repercussions on a healthy and effective turnover in the executive classes.

Downstream from this brief list of criteria that determine how every university is positioned, we must underline two points. The first point, which we alluded to

Strategic choices for universities of science and technology **121**

early on, is the need to frame these individual choices within educational systems where the vocations vary. In Europe, as we have noted, technical education is generally taught at universities for the masses, and the quality is good or excellent. Any substantial discontinuity in the choices made by these universities individually must be read against the background of system-wide features. The second point, also important, is that universities with a large number of students must balance the need to provide high standards in teaching for the many against the need to produce exemplary research, which is evermore relevant in today's changed competitive landscape.

Combining the two facets, education essentially for the masses, in a European model of technical and scientific teaching, and the requirement to put the spotlight on people and areas of excellence, is a possibility that could be achieved by diversifying the offer within single universities through paths or schools set apart for the students with the greatest potential. There is also another valid point linked to the availability of resources and the relationship between professor and student. Wealthier universities (or those better off than the average university in their countries) may find it easier to cultivate their talented students in small classes, giving them a different range of activities, even when student numbers are high overall.

4.3 System – choosing the organization model

We have outlined up to here, the possible trends in technical universities for creating and spreading knowledge, and how relationships with other actors are managed, within the international landscape and as part of the path of growth for their people, be they students, teaching or non-teaching staff. The way a university defines the boundaries of its operations and how it places itself in relation to people will influence how knowledge is created and diffused. The third point to consider when planning for the future of universities is the university system, that is, understanding how they will operate and what organizational model they will adopt to generate and spread knowledge, together with how relationships are managed within the institutional and human spheres.

The long history of universities means that it is particularly difficult to isolate ideal organizational models because the references that we are looking at today are the outcome of university systems adapting over time to the specific economic, cultural, and social context that shaped them and where they evolved. However, starting from the ongoing trends and the processes of transformation initiated in many situations, we can describe several ideal types of governance that summarize the possible trajectories of evolution for universities. These models will typically differ in the organization's architecture and the configuration of its components. On the one side, the single functions (teaching, research) may be structured vertically and the organizational units (schools, departments, etc.) be ordered into hierarchical decision chains, all connected to a central control hub. On the other side, there may be a more horizontal structure, where individual organizational units enjoy greater autonomy and responsibility, and control is exerted through shared values, the consensus in setting strategies and objectives, and interdisciplinary mechanisms of coordination and collaboration.

We can describe the organizational and management models along four different lines:

- The system of external constraints, where legal and bureaucratic issues can influence the organization; in other words, the possibility of implementing models that give more or less autonomy and control.
- The architecture proper of the organization for primary functions and organizational units, their hierarchical relationships and relative duties and responsibilities.
- The structure in place for decision-making processes, which oversee the way the organization functions, as well as how well it can adapt to the context or to radical change.
- The organization and management of human resources and level of HR specialization and/or HR competencies integrated within primary functions and services.

After analysing these four lines, we can identify several opposing directions that can ideally describe the possible strategic choices that can be enacted within a particular governance model.

4.3.1 Constraints of context and type of organization: autonomy or control

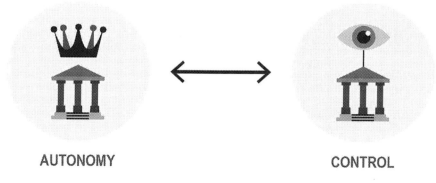

AUTONOMY   CONTROL

The debate on the models of governance in universities often hinges on the centrality of the public–private dichotomy, giving the impression that a greater or lesser public or private shareholding could be one of the most significant aspects that shape a university and its organizational model. Furthermore, this impression leads to the assumption that the differentiation could become even more marked in the future, especially in contexts where resources are diminishing. In reality, university systems have evolved and will evolve in a more layered and multifaceted fashion, with two distinct planes, one for ownership and one for the level of control exerted by the local or central governments. Today, there are totally autonomous private universities and private universities under public control. In the United States and Japan, roughly three-quarters of all universities are private and are in essence completely autonomous. On the contrary, a number of private universities in Italy and the *Grandes Écoles* in France are nevertheless under strict government overview.

Similarly, some public universities are subject to stringent norms and procedures and others enjoy varying degrees of autonomy. The first case is the prevalent model in Europe and China, where most decisions are constrained by policies defined centrally or locally. The second, instead, is the situation in the United Kingdom and Switzerland, or indeed in Singapore, where universities are generally public but mostly make their own decisions. While there are many possible models, their common trait, which must be consolidated, is to see the university system as a vital component in any model of advanced civil society, and as such should be at the heart of all development policies in all national economies. If we start from this premise, the main thread running through all feasible organizational models is not the distinction between public and private, but how a public system can steer its university policies, potentially also adopting hybrid models that work best in a specific context. The more governments can invest in education, research and innovation, the greater will be their inclination to control the university system. Vice versa, when a government's investment in the university system drops, it must inevitably then concede greater autonomy to universities and open the doors to public–private models.

In the specific case of high control, it can be exerted at different levels and so will impact the system in different ways. When such control is at central government level, as is the case today in France and Italy, the restrictions faced by universities are determined by the desire for across-the-board standards. When, instead, high control is exerted at a regional or provincial level, as today in Germany and China, universities will be expected to comply with regulations that arise from more specific local interests. The size and population of each country also come into play.

In future, single universities, public and private alike, will find themselves having to negotiate their level of autonomy within local or central government policies, in function of the benefits they may gain. We can identify at least six broad areas of autonomy:

- *Statutes and organization*: universities define their governance bodies and organizational structure autonomously, according to their mission and objectives.

124 Strategic choices for universities of science and technology

- *Economics and finances*: universities manage their assets, accounts and financial flows autonomously.
- *Personnel*: universities have autonomy in managing all processes linked to recruitment, size and development of teaching and non-teaching staff.
- *Administration*: universities manage all administrative processes (e.g. purchasing, infrastructures, professional appointments) along the same lines as in the private sector.
- *Teaching and the right to study*: universities are autonomous in defining their study programmes, setting student fees and awarding grants and scholarships.
- *Research and innovation*: research lines and policies of innovation and technological transfer are defined autonomously by each university.

We must also keep in mind the benefits and disadvantages of greater autonomy and greater control.

Greater autonomy does not automatically imply more benefits than government control. One obvious benefit is that when universities can spend their resources more freely, they will be able to compete more effectively in a progressively more competitive world. Other areas will be affected as a consequence, such as the universities' policies to attract a higher standard of students, professors and other personnel. They will also be able to introduce forms of organization and new teaching programmes less closely bound to central legislative tools, as well as implementing leaner administration and management procedures. They will be able to invest in new research lines not necessarily imposed from above and set their own evaluation parameters and measure results against objectives as they are needed.

Greater autonomy also opens them up to greater risks of bad management. Autonomy in the areas of statutes and organization, in the financial sphere and in administrative processes brings with it the potential risk of non-virtuous universities heading for demise when they are unsustainable in the long term. University autonomy in policies linked to personnel management could, for example, imply the need to abolish the concept of *tenure*, today a typical feature in nearly every public university, if incorrect choices should be made about staff size and career progression. Total autonomy in teaching and research could have some, albeit less serious, implications on an individual university, and indirectly weaken its sustainability over time.

On the contrary, greater control, centrally or locally, ensures stability in operational processes and economic and financial sustainability, deriving from its public sector coverage. Government oversight tends to compensate for the negative impact of risky decisions made by single universities and left unresolved, even, in extreme cases, covering losses arising from bad management. Furthermore, decisions taken at government level drive the universities' actions, without them continuously having to outline their policies for future development; this does create a more monochromatic system, but it also ensures the same quality standards throughout.

Greater control, however, can produce the typical consequences of an overly bureaucratic public administration, where the apparatus has to respond to general rules conceived for very diverse services (ranging from universities to transport). Firstly, excessive stability and public underwriting tend to induce opportunistic behaviour on the part of institutions and even individuals, within a system geared more towards standardization and the lowest common denominator type of quality, reflecting the weaker or disadvantaged organizations, rather than driving growth where there is potential. In the long term, this mechanism will tend to flatten out the system, with single universities becoming more static and sometimes creating an atmosphere of general demotivation among teaching and non-teaching staff. This situation is more likely to occur where money is tight and lower salaries are not proportional to the level of responsibility, social role and commitment demanded from personnel. In conclusion, greater external control, especially in contexts affected by recession, tends to drastically reduce the possibility of innovation in individual universities and their capacity to move rapidly in response to environmental stimuli.

Remaining on the topic of control, we have already mentioned the concept of "steering at a distance" and the use of indicators to guide university policies. In the future, the realization will sink in across the world that using indicators common to all the universities in a single system produces over-homogenization without giving universities the means to differentiate themselves for their distinctive expertise. Even in models involving some degree of control, and thus where universities are not autonomous, it will be necessary to set clear development policies that reflect each university's specific features and local area. Therefore, results will be measured through indicators appropriate to each case.

Another element to examine within this framework is the continuing development of structures external to the universities; these foundations, consortia and satellite associations have the task of injecting the necessary flexibility within universities unable to invest along their desired lines due to government restrictions. Suitable governance mechanisms must, in any case, be put in place such that the external entities act in coherence and alignment with the university's strategy, as there is the risk that, over time, they could secure a form of operational independence, overlapping the university's designs in a sort of internal competition.

Very briefly, on the one side all the benefits linked to greater autonomy must be balanced against the loss of warranty mechanisms that are typical of subjects under public control, and, on the other, the stability procured by a controlling government must be juxtaposed against needless rigidity and the problems of competing on an international stage.

4.3.2 Architecture: one-dimension or multi-dimension

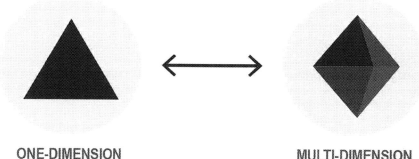

ONE-DIMENSION   MULTI-DIMENSION

Alongside the various degrees of autonomy and public holdings in academic institutions, the organizational arrangements in universities can also vary. The long history of universities means that they have assembled an extensive array of organizational models, the outcome of processes to transform and adapt to the social, cultural and economic landscapes in which they are embedded and where they have evolved. We can, nevertheless, extrapolate two archetypes where the universities' primary functions (teaching, research, entrepreneurship and innovation, and impact on society) are configured according to a one-dimension or multi-dimension logic.

A one-dimension organization is when the university's primary functions are ordered in a hierarchy, where one in particular (e.g. teaching or research) gives origin to the organizational units that oversee the others (in many universities across the world, these are the schools, to which the departments and other facilities are then bolted). The leading units generally cover an extensive range of thematic interests and are medium to large in size; they have representation in the university's main governance bodies and take part in decisions on strategies and allocating resources.

The benefits of this model make it effective even within contexts pinned down by regulations and dwindling resources. Organizational processes, in particular, flow more linearly and efficiently, and decision-making processes are simpler. When only the primary organizational units are represented on the central bodies, the implementation of strategic lines agreed at the university level are devolved to the units themselves, which can have the autonomy to make their own decisions in some areas, such as recruitment. In this model, where one unit coordinates the others, specific functions (for instance research), can be prioritized when strategies are being defined; in part, the objective is to optimize the parameters for evaluating

Strategic choices for universities of science and technology **127**

and rewarding performance that define the specific context and national economy. The structure of this model can also be explained more simply to the external world, with the advantage of determining and strengthening the university's identity through a few operational lines and topics. Finally, this arrangement caters for a more organic type of control and is open to highly specialized functions within each unit.

On the flip side, according to the scope and features of the functions in play, the one-dimension model has some limits in its ability to exploit certain processes and skills university-wide, or to set up channels of interdisciplinary inter-functional sharing. In particular, the main units tend to see their processes in a vertical perspective, firming up a model of ordering knowledge into stand-alone self-contained silos, which tends to dissuade cooperation among different fields. Added to this is the general propensity for the various areas to develop their teaching and research strategies internally, in response to demands from the outside world and current trends. This is typically the case when new complex and strategic topics enter the scene (e.g. AI, biotech, smart cities, etc.), and each unit is liable to respond with its own resources, doubling up skills and omitting to tap into the full potential in the organization by not approaching things with a multi-disciplinary and overarching eye. As a final point, especially when considering aspects such as public engagement and life-long learning, the one-dimension model is apt to generate initiatives locked into the single organizational units, generating redundancy and overlapping topics.

In the opposite corner, the organizational setup that arranges matters according to a multi-dimension logic is more likely to introduce a federal type of structure in the units that oversee the university's primary functions (teaching, research, entrepreneurship and innovation, and impact on society). In this model, all the functional areas are represented centrally in the university's deciding bodies, participating equally in defining strategies and allocating resources. The multi-dimensional arrangement has advantages that make it particularly effective in harmonizing strategies to the needs of the various academic elements, especially teaching and research. The domain of teaching is configured to be more open to participation among the various subject fields and so more capable of elaborating programmes on multi-disciplinary and transdisciplinary topics. This situation can be advanced through more autonomous education cycles (e.g. setting up a graduate school for master's and PhD programmes), which do not necessarily follow a logic of continuity.

Within research, a multi-dimensional arrangement can take the form of a hybrid structure with small research groups (or departments) that specialize exclusively in their subject, alongside research centres (or institutes) with a wider discipline focus often centred on emerging topics (AI, biotech) or which are closely identified with the university. Research can thus include a model "by disciplines" reporting to the departments and a model "by projects" reporting to the institutes, which cooperate with all the departments, thereby ensuring adequate discipline coverage and a scale sufficiently large to handle wide-scope research topics. This model also has the advantage of being able to organize other activities such as continuous learning and public engagement, which can run across all the organizational units, tapping into all the elements and avoiding overlaps and redundancies.

On the downside, the multi-dimension model has limits that mainly concern complexity in organizational and decision-making processes. In particular, as the functions are not set up in a hierarchical order, teaching and research strategies must be fully integrated, often introducing conflicts induced by the levels of autonomy in the various research groups or single organizational units, especially apropos the allocation of resources and recruitment processes. Defining the system of relationships and interdependencies among all the units (schools, departments, and institutes) is also arduous and consequently so is the configuration of an efficient and uniform model for managing and organizing the teaching body and the technical and administrative staff.

The complexity of the great challenges that universities will face and the rapid pace of advances in technology will tend to favour universities with small and agile organizational units that interact together on objectives and specific projects. These networks of interaction and collaboration can be internal and external to the individual universities.

4.3.3 Decision-making procedures and resource allocation: direct or indirect

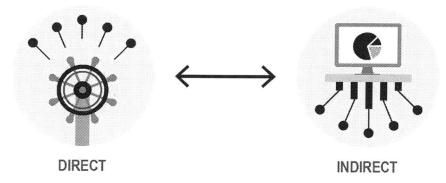

Alongside the form of organization, another major dimension in defining a governance model is how decisional processes are structured, especially when elaborating strategies and allocating the resources necessary to take them forward. University organizations must give themselves the objective of harmonizing the current management of their operations with the development of new strategies.

In other words, they must be able to ensure continuity in their services (teaching offer, research, third mission and the infrastructure underpinning them). Equally, they must be able to develop new strategies and constantly transform themselves to address continued change in knowledge and the growing complexity of future challenges, both for the profiles that are moulded and for the potential impact of their research and technological transfer. This last objective brings with it the need to renew and upgrade infrastructure and resources in a logic of continuous evolution. Pursuing these two objectives, ensuring that everything works as it should and that everything is transformed when it needs to, is closely influenced by how decision-making processes are structured and, on this basis, determine two archetypes, the normative model and the prescriptive model.

The normative, or indirect method is based on an arrangement that encourages efficiency and effectiveness in ordinary management, so that resources are allocated on the basis of criteria defined beforehand and delegating decision-making on specific strategies to the individual organizational units, that is, to departments, schools, institutes, course of study, etc. Within this context, the mechanisms that ensure continuity and a working operation, namely, the allocation of resources, must take priority over defining or redefining sweeping and disruptive strategies concerning the direction to be taken by the university. The decisions linked to these mechanisms must be agreed upon and shared by all those with senior positions in the units and the organization, and be based on parameters and indicators that can be used to measure performance in single units against specific benchmarks. For example, if a university wants to expand its research into artificial intelligence, it will define how to split resources that reward anyone in the organization who gets scientific results (papers published, for instance) in this field.

Such a model based on parameters underpinning resource allocation has the great plus point of reducing conflicts and complexity when decisions are taken, smoothing day-by-day management with more efficient and effective processes. Another benefit is that the units enjoy high autonomy and, compatibly with their resources, they can make local decisions about their choice of direction in teaching, research and third mission. In terms of strategic capability, this model can steer an organization by leveraging on the parameters chosen as performance indicators for the various functions and set criteria with a rewarding element that are applied when allocating resources. Finally, taking a national economy perspective, if designed correctly, this model could be used to set out coherent development strategies for the university system in its entirety, achieved through the actions of the various individual universities, their units and their research teams.

A model of this kind obviously requires a certain homogeneity in assessing the various organizational units and this is not always a given, especially in universities with great internal diversity. For instance, if we look at bibliometric indicators, it is a known fact that they cannot all be applied in the same way and with the same

130 Strategic choices for universities of science and technology

weighting to subjects that are very different from one another. Furthermore, this model will tend to consolidate the organization, as the changes induced are slow and adaptive, either if promoted at central level or by the individual units (single schools, departments, study courses, etc.), and it does not encourage the type of radical change that must be backed by specific strategies set centrally or locally and not always in continuity with the past. This strategic inertia is even more pronounced when parameters defined centrally are replicated to the letter at all levels of the organization.

Finally, in parallel with all management control systems based on measuring indicators, the normative model is in danger of generating calculating and devious conduct unless the parameters are defined extremely carefully. In defining the parameters for rewarding performance or allocating resources, we must always ask ourselves how they will influence the behaviour of people working within the organization. For example, if one of the criteria to allocate resources is the number of students taught by each faculty member, which is a perfectly logical assumption, we must also be aware that it will inevitably affect the way that the educational offer is designed, and this in turn will distract some attention away from professional roles, student needs and necessary skills.

The prescriptive or direct model is based on configuring the university's decisional processes so that its decision-making bodies have wide freedom to make choices about its strategic guidelines and on how it allocates resources to implement its ensuing strategic objectives. In this model, foresight and vision come first, along with elaborating guideline strategies for the various functions within the university, and the mechanisms to allocate resources are subordinated to the strategic decisions. In a context where it is necessary to make a clear-cut distinction between resources to be used for ordinary business, which can be distributed according to criteria that need not be connected to performance parameters (e.g. size-related parameters), and resources for investment purposes.

Investment resources can be allocated very unevenly to the various university components on the basis of strategic decisions about the potential growth of some areas compared to others, or to back special projects or completely new initiatives. This model reduces the units' individual autonomy for making decisions about development strategies, as they must inevitably direct their proposals for change to the centre, and thus build a consensus for strategic directions and the ensuing investment. Going back to the previous example of a university that wants to expand its research into artificial intelligence, the expectation within this model would be to allocate conspicuous resources to create a new AI research centre or attract AI stars from all over the world.

The prescriptive model has the great benefit of giving large-scale complex organizations the capacity to make even radical changes, selecting, from among a range of proposals, the most promising for the overall strategic vision and the contextual conditions. Operating in a logic steered towards strategic change, this model could anchor decisional processes more securely to qualitative and peer-to-peer assessment criteria. Apart from centrally defined grand transformation strategies, it could be possible to encourage proposals from single functional areas like departments, schools, study courses and research centres, selected on the basis of peer-to-peer qualitative assessment and then supported through funds sufficient for their implementation. Compared to allocation dictated by quantitative criteria, as in the previous model, this model can cater for change on a much larger scale and of greater impact. On the downside, the prescriptive model is more risky, as wrong decisions about discontinuity with the past could determine massive losses and be difficult to reverse. It is also obvious that decisional processes would be more fraught and could heighten internal competition among the various academic components with negative outcomes, especially where resources are stationary or decreasing.

Very briefly, both models have many advantages and they both hide pitfalls. It may even be the case that the two models could coexist within a virtuous university that knows how to plan for its future. A university could prioritize a basic normative approach but earmark part of its resources to launch new projects and initiatives. Or it could follow a totally prescriptive approach to research, backing new research centres on a case-by-case basis and expecting them to stand on their own two feet after their start-up phase, while, at the same time, it would be normative in allocating its teaching resources.

4.3.4 Human resource organization and management: specialization or integration

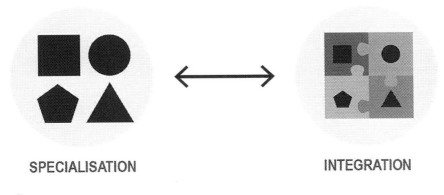

As we have seen, one of the most discussed topics of the past years is the role played by the size of a university's technical-administrative side. The university world has generally gone through a transition from a model of academic adhocracy, where universities were managed by faculty in a more or less collegiate arrangement, to a university-company model, inspired by the principles of *new public management*, with the technical and administrative sphere gaining in importance.

The juxtaposition between academic and administrative perspectives cannot be a real alternative in the light of the changes that have already taken place because the complexity and scale of most universities are no longer compatible with a management model based exclusively on academic expertise. The more complex an organization is and the more challenging the environment where it operates, the more necessary it is for them to have a management setup that can go beyond simple technical and administrative business. Universities must have a vision for future development, define projects and actions to be implemented, find and allocate the necessary resources for their strategic plans, be able to complete these initiatives and, last but not least, manage paths for HR development and motivation, which are fundamental for achieving any given objective. All this implies that the university can field the expertise to do this, to make a fundamental cultural change from a logic of "current administration" to a logic of "strategic management", regardless of where such expertise comes from, be it technical and administrative staff, teaching or research faculty. Universities that can grow on today's stage, competing in an international teaching and research world with evermore complex challenges, must necessarily bring together specific and specialist skills, in a viewpoint of strategic organization and management.

When defining the alternative models, the first option is a requalification and empowerment of the professional side of management, with non-academic personnel developing a constructive set of management skills alongside those on the technical and administrative side. The second option is an integrated model, where faculty develop their management skills, potentially through purposely designed career programmes covering strategic management.

The first option, probably the most common among international universities, involves progressively more distinctive professional roles and leads to the vertical specialization of skills. Professors and researchers are only concerned with teaching or research and innovation, and their time and attention are not diverted to organization and management matters. This choice tends to encourage specialization in core university functions, with potential benefits in terms of academic productivity. Concurrently, much work is needed to give universities the expertise to manage their organizational, technical and administrative facet in a highly professional way. The boundary between these two professional worlds must be very clear in a university following this model. The skills belonging to the non-academic faction could finish up by being restricted to the finance and economic sphere alone, or to HR management, or even to drawing up projects for competitive calls and helping to delineate future settings in education and research.

The potential risk of this course of action is further divergence between the two sides. The academic body could become entrenched on one side, busy

Strategic choices for universities of science and technology **133**

carrying out its scientific objectives in total freedom, while the management brigade is ensconced on the other, concerned with the university's objectives of efficiency and efficacy as such, without finding the way to give adequate support to its primary missions of teaching and scientific research. Planning, at all levels, suitable organizational mechanisms to bridge the two sides becomes a fundamental step, and they must face each other as equals and share the organization's overall strategic objectives (sharing information, coordination meetings, incentive schemes and staff assessment procedures). This arrangement is valid for the board of directors, the academic senate, the schools, departments, down to the single organizational units. Both sides of the organization must be planned as part of an integrated system, and roles and skills for people at the same level must be given clear and equal standing.

In the second option, the university's academic component takes on all management functions, especially those concerning strategy, in accordance with the mentality of the individual people and their previous experience in organizational roles. Professors and researchers who have a bent for and interest in the management side of a university could be involved in major organizational operations (e.g. communication, student management, human resources, agreements with other universities) and build career paths that gradually reduce their exposure to teaching and research. In parallel, they could expand their management and strategic skills, including through courses and training.

At its basis, the second model gives the academic body more autonomy in personalizing individual development paths, with the option of greater specialization in various university functions, and has the benefit of endorsing the value of personal skills and aptitude in professors who could choose a career that is on par with one in teaching or research. Some academics could refocus on teaching or research; others could prefer management roles and concentrate on acquiring a management skillset. The further plus point is an organic integration between the organizational processes and the requirements of the teaching, scientific and innovation sphere, tapping into the knowledge and expertise in these areas assembled within the "management" academic body.

In this second model, non-academic functions act primarily as technical and operational support to the academic component and have no decisional autonomy, a factor that could lead to a de-qualification of technical functions over time. Another risk is that the university's academic productivity could be undermined by the fact that part of the academic body is not fully engaged in research or teaching. Furthermore, management-type academic careers over time tend to create professions per se and could induce the manager-professors to transit between universities and make choices that are not necessarily long term. Finally, leaving university management solely in the hands of professors and researchers could introduce risks deriving from improvisation on the manager front, when in fact the responsibilities should need to be well bedded in experience and virtuosity.

To sum up, the challenge between greater or lesser separation between academic and management careers, and for professional specialization, is connected to whether universities can build mechanisms whereby people can choose and personalize their paths of professional growth, and whether the institutions can implement transparent tools to assess competencies and results. Their success in this undertaking could be the trigger that will motivate professors and other staff to achieve assured and predictable results in the medium to long term.

Chapter references

Agasisti, T. et al. (2018). "Academic resilience: What schools and countries do to help disadvantaged students succeed in PISA", OECD Education Working Papers, No. 167, OECD Publishing, Paris.

Aghion, P., Dewatripont, M., Hoxby, C., Mas-Colell, A., & Sapir, A. (2010). The governance and performance of universities: Evidence from Europe and the US. *Economic Policy*, 25(61), 7–59.

Bonaccorsi A., Haddawy, P., Cicero, T., & Hassan, S. U. (2017). The solitude of stars: An analysis of the distributed excellence model of European universities. *Journal of Informetrics*, 11, 435–454.

Fassbinder, A. G., Fassbinder, M., & Barbosa, E. F. (2015). From flipped classroom theory to the personalized design of learning experiences in MOOCs. In *IEEE Frontiers in Education Conference (FIE)*, El Paso, TX.

Flexner, A. (2017). *The usefulness of useless knowledge*. Cambridge, MA: Harvard University Press.

Gibbons, M., Nowotny, H., Schwartzman, S., Scott, P., & Trow, M. (1994). *The new production of knowledge*. Thousand Oaks, CA: SAGE Publications.

Mitchell, K. (2012). Student mobility and European identity: Erasmus study as a civic experience? *Journal of Contemporary European Research*, 8(4).

Narayanamurti, V., & Odumosu, T. (2016). *Cycles of invention and discovery: Rethinking the endless frontier*. Cambridge, MA: Harvard University Press.

Russo, L. (2008). *La cultura componibile. Dalla frammentazione alla disgregazione del sapere*. Naples, Italy: Liguori Editore.

Sancassani, S. (2019). *Progettare l'innovazione didattica*. Milan, Italy: Pearson Italia.

Selingo, J. J. (2014, October 29). Demystifying the MOOC. *The New York Times*. https://www.nytimes.com/2014/11/02/education/edlife/demystifying-the-mooc.html

Stiglitz, J. E., & Greenwald, B. (2014). *Creating a learning society: A new approach to growth, development, and social progress*. New York, NY: Columbia University Press.

Varghese, N. V. (2008). *Globalization of higher education and cross-border student mobility*. Paris, France: UNESCO International Institute for Educational Planning.

5
CONCLUSIONS

This book gives an overview of the strategic decisions that universities must contend with over the upcoming years; it does not purport to be exhaustive but will simply highlight and analyse some of the paths that universities may decide to venture along in the future. Some of the dynamics involved will no doubt have been accelerated by Covid-19, but the trajectories of evolution were already up and running before the pandemic. The chosen strategic directions must, in any case, be coherent with each other, whilst also reflecting developments in the context of reference.

5.1 Coherence within strategic decisions

A university that decides to embark on a path of super specialization, investing heavily in a few subjects to stake their claim to an international leadership position in these fields, must manoeuvre its levers in a concerted manner. In our increasingly interconnected world, where global challenges must be faced from all sides and many skills fielded, we must envisage formal cooperation mechanisms whereby networks of complementary universities can share their expertise and academic courses. This arrangement could be strengthened by developing digital tools for continuous collaboration in teaching and in research. Scientific leadership also consists of being able to see the next pioneering topic ahead of the general debate and be ready to invest in it; in other words, a university must know how to galvanize prominence for its research projects. This process is probably associated with knowing how to attract international research celebrities and operating through a simple and one-dimensional organizational system, ordered by chairs or subjects and based on crystal clear objectives and merit, with a good dose of autonomy in managing its resources.

DOI: 10.4324/9781003231004-06

136 Conclusions

On the contrary, a university aspiring to build up its selection of competences and work on internal subject cross-fertilization will take other decisions. It will depend less on international networks and alliances to complement its own expertise and will be more independent and self-reliant in its teaching and research. Its research projects will tap into home-grown multi-disciplinary teams rather than attracting international personalities, and it will use digital tools to support and improve events held in presence. Its organizational structure will have to be sophisticated enough to handle the breadth of the research topics in which it is engaged. It is easy to see it branch out into cross-departmental research centres and study programmes, more concerned with the common topic than a common subject.

Should a university want to contribute to society by training and developing researchers and other people who can make a strong impact on the future, then it must think along these lines when making decisions. It will need to select its students, professors and researchers with extreme care, subjecting them to rigorous and demanding development processes, and ultimately either moulding or attracting international names in research. These people will be expected to contribute individually to pioneering research topics and so further consolidate the university's reputation. To be able to offer personalized development programmes to the most talented people, based on contacts, relationships and their ongoing physical presence, the selection criteria will inevitably have to factor in the available resources. A policy of this kind would, of course, have to be backed by decisive management autonomy, enabling a university to stand up to government policies should they oppose this direction of development.

Conversely, should a university want to contribute to society by raising standards in education and culture on a wide scale, it will make other decisions. It will open its doors to a progressively larger intake of students, teaching staff and researchers, who will embark primarily on standard programmes and achieve a good level of knowledge and ability. It will use digital tools to expand its offer further and will reach and connect with a wider number of people. Research and scientific production will harness the power of a pool brimming with teams and people. Development of this kind could work within a situation of lesser management autonomy matched by government control, focused on the comprehensive social objective of raising the level of education throughout the country.

5.2 Influence of the context of reference

Some of these considerations can draw attention to the role played by several contextual variables that must be taken into account when defining a development strategy. Even the universities on a global trajectory that goes beyond national boundaries will have to reckon with the local and international setting in which they operate. They will not necessarily have to stand by and passively submit to the influences of their surrounding area, but it may require a university-wide effort to affect and modify their own environment, making it possible for them to establish their own position and strategic plan. The factors to take into account are

Conclusions **137**

international geopolitical dynamics, the local government setup, the social and economic system of reference and available resources.

We covered the geopolitical dynamics currently running through the research world in the early chapters of this text. One trend underway for years, which will probably continue to run on, is the global competition between the United States and China for leadership in research and technological development. These two countries are dominating the world stage, in terms of GDP, growth and technological innovation. Both the United States and China have a strong national identity (*"American Dream"* and *"My Mother China"*), and the ability to work as a system and create synergy. They also have a substantial critical mass, making them capable of guiding technological development. In these settings, the universities that will benefit most, in both the private and public sector, are those willing to invest in scientific excellence and on attracting international talent, thereby pushing the boundaries of research, even when they are operating autonomously.

In this framework, the European Union could be a significant third player in the global challenge. The drawback is that it is suffering from the consequences of policies implemented at the backend of the last century and from recent economic downturns, meaning that it has come to a deadlock, buffered by centrifugal forces that occasionally ferment drives for nationalism. In the long term, the EU's power will inevitably lie in its ability to set out clear policies for "human and sustainable" technological development, and to establish a sort of balance point for the entire world rooted in its own values, which stem from its history, and are adduced as fundamental and complementary to the value systems in the United States and China:

- *Diversity and complementarity*: our European history is a rich tapestry of quite different cultures, in the past often in conflict, which have enjoyed a few decades of peace and integration. This will allow us to appreciate the differences and the richness that derives from their complementary features.
- *Mental openness and mutual respect*: European culture is generally defined by respect for the person, support, and knowing how to listen and see a problem from different angles.
- *Capacity for analysis and critical thinking*: being able to engage in reflective and independent thinking, after carefully examining the question at hand, is a pivotal element in the process of contributing positively to technological development at the service of humanity.
- *Centrality of the person*: the value of the person above all is the defining element throughout much of philosophical thought in Europe.
- *Entrepreneurship and innovation*: Europe has been the source of great innovation in bygone centuries, today it is experiencing the charge of other geographical regions. It must recover its historical and intrinsic capacity for innovation, not just through new business, but also by changing the modus operandi of existing organizations.

138 Conclusions

In Europe, universities will find more space for strategic networks and alliances that outstrip by far the networks and alliances we know today, and which will know how to share complementary assets and resources. We will see people moving between universities and between countries without barriers or bureaucratic hassle. We will see digital platforms that can permanently connect students, professors and researchers from different universities. The seeds of this script can be glimpsed in the *European University Initiative*, a project recently launched by the EU that will take years to come to fruition.

Even the local political and government environment, in the single countries and regions, can express powers that will influence university development. Starting from one of the basic assumptions in this book, namely that education and scientific and technological development will always be at the root of the economy in the more advanced countries, progress can potentially be pursued through a number of government policies. Some countries will adopt undifferentiated policies that focus on continuously raising the level of education among the population, and so will induce universities to expand their work and increase students and staff, compatibly with available resources (more on this later). Other countries will instead introduce differentiated policies that cater for local variations, and will, for example, persuade some universities to address the need for increasing the general level of education and run training sessions on a grand scale; elsewhere, universities will be encouraged to pursue scientific excellence underpinned by carefully selected topics and people (students and researchers) at an international level.

Clearly, when taking strategic decisions, universities will be influenced by the current government policies. In the first case, universities will ready themselves to manage research projects that have a direct impact on their local area, without feeling that they must chase the most pioneering topics and, with a larger number of students to teach, will use digital tools more extensively. Everything will be well ordered and coordinated, to secure a reasonably uniform university system countrywide. In the second case, the different types of universities will gradually diverge, and each university will have a distinct role within its own ecosystem. Some universities will be encouraged to focus prevalently on training, possibly working in partnership with their reference industrial system, drawing on teams of teaching staff and linking their identity to specific topics and subjects; they will procure advanced digital tools to reach greater numbers of students. Other universities will, instead, pursue scientific excellence, transferring part of their resources from teaching to research, and will try to attract international research celebrities, focus on ground-breaking themes and establish connections with globally acclaimed universities and research centres.

Another factor that will influence university policies is their social and economic system of reference. During the 2020 health crisis, there was much talk of experts and expertise, and scientific and technological progress was at the centre of world attention and debate. During a crisis, it is natural to emphasize the role of science and research; all too often, however, once the crisis is over, research and innovation tend to be put on the backburner within society's value system. In a

Conclusions 139

future marked by intense technological development, the front line will be occupied by social-economic and industrial systems that can marry up technological progress and the development of skills.

The more companies and the public believe and invest in science and education (seeing them as drivers of social progress) and the more they see the academic world as an engine for growth and social wellbeing, the more universities will be in a position to invest in pioneering research. They will be able to attract highly qualified people from anywhere in the world and be free to determine their direction for development and how they manage their resources. Universities will have to earn this place and demonstrate very clearly that they can have a positive impact on society, without running the risk of once more being seen as ivory towers detached from reality.

Should, instead, the social and economic system, companies and the public fail to place their trust in the academic system as the motor to drive social progress, then the opportunities for universities to develop would be lost. The industrial system of reference, and the people affected, would see universities mainly as a kind of supplier selling skills with an immediate return for the world of work. In this setting, the policies in many universities would be to bolster their teaching side, using standard programmes to turn out graduates with the skills demanded in the job market, and resorting to digital tools to increase training effectiveness and efficiency. It would be more difficult for universities to stand out as points of reference in trailblazing research on the international stage, and they would have to rely on close-knit teams of competent people, without feeling the need to attract new talent capable of opening new research topics.

Finally, all the factors so far mentioned converge on a final point that will influence strategic development in all universities: whether the necessary resources are available.

First of all, international geopolitical dynamics, government policies and the culture in the reference social-economic and industrial systems will determine the volume and destination of the funding needed for them to develop. The powers that be will have to believe in the university system and invest enormous sums to support scientific and technological progress and so reward universities that create and propagate innovation. The more they do so, the more universities will have the resources they need to pull all the levers that enable them to set themselves apart on the international stage and decide where to invest in the long term. On the contrary, wherever resources earmarked for the university system are tight, the development will inevitably be modest and restricted to what is needed in the short and medium term.

Secondly, every university will have to factor in its own history, the skills developed within and the people available. For a university to change its strategic position, shifting its stance, for instance, from a university with a large number of students and mainly concerned with the teaching side to a more selective advanced research university, or vice versa, is not simple and would need to be backed by multi-year investments that would only give a future return. Investments designed

140 Conclusions

to bring about cultural change across the entire organization, would, in turn, alter recruitment policies, usher in a different way of managing people and generate investment in new spaces and equipment.

As we have pointed out previously, the contextual factors mentioned will certainly affect future development in the university system, but they must not be taken as inevitable rigid constraints. A clear strategic vision to steer a university's development could include, if possible and not unrealistic, the effort of partially changing one or more of the contextual factors.

5.3 Potential discontinuity

These context-linked elements restrict and influence choices relating to the main decisional levers covered in Section 5.2. Their "dampening" effect creates inertia to change, meaning that, although the pace of change is faster than in the past, each university can take informed control over its lines of evolution.

There are, however, sets of circumstances where these levers can be manoeuvred at greater speed, as well as on the basis of disruptive choices that break with the past. When we started to research and analyse material for this book, we came up against the difficulty of conjuring up situations of discontinuity in the university system, and the risk of making predictions that would be at odds with reality. Covid-19 then offered us the chance to "never let a good crisis go to waste"; we could see which variables, in a system under immense stress, would be influenced more and could determine real change when stimulated by the need to respond to the risks highlighted by the pandemic and to the opportunities for innovation engendered by what was being labelled by Giaccardi and Magatti (2020) as a "vital catastrophe".

This backdrop for change could hardly have been dreamt up before the pandemic, and now it is extremely likely that we will see the rise of totally online university education, digital from beginning to end, that could even be offered by distinguished international universities. While this offer will not and cannot replace the traditional experience of a university town or campus, in the universities that decide to propose this option, it will nevertheless radically change all the aspects linked to "relationships" discussed in Chapter 4 and some of those linked to the overall "system". It is clear that this type of proposal may be a response to the difficulty or impossibility of students travelling caused by the pandemic, but it is also true that we could expect to see changes in the international flows of students because of the slow de-globalization triggered by protectionism policies, the growing weight of China in technological progress and local circumstances such as Brexit.

The landscape of change in technologies and professions, a topic that we have covered extensively in previous chapters, may be setting the scene to give distance university education a role only hinted at until now. The job market is increasingly demanding high specialist skills, no longer just in medium-high professional

Conclusions **141**

positions, but also in the mass of jobs previously calling for much lower qualifications. Traditional university programmes, explicitly in technical and scientific universities or faculties, tend to be selective and expensive. They are also able to train people with high critical thinking and interpersonal skills, who generally have great professional expectations. There is now space in the market for delivering the micro-skills arising from technological progress to a much wider audience of students, who could be the bedrock of the future workforce. This space could be occupied by universities taking choices of discontinuity with their past, and by totally new entrants. The newcomers to this market will likely include global technology corporations (known as the big tech companies), which are certainly feeling the need for a wide array of professional skills that enable a vast audience of people to navigate through code development, data elaboration algorithms, AI applications, new production technologies and so forth. Google has already announced its short online university courses; other organizations, having shown their development flair in the production of training material, will probably follow suit.

The drive to bring a large swathe of people up to university level education can induce countries to make choices that will have major impacts on the entire country and its university system. To avoid becoming marginalized in the global economic race, countries with resources matching the size of the undertaking may choose to redesign their system to give everyone a university education, for example, by raising school-leaving age. Such a decision would obviously have a massive effect on all the strategic levers in the universities involved, as they would have to review all the variables in the system relating to the organization plus all those concerning relationships. Raising the level of education of a country's entire population could potentially be beneficial in the long term, especially in the field of innovation. However, generating knowledge through scientific research, traditionally a university function, could suffer because energies would be diverted to the primary task of teaching. Conversely, choices along these lines could attract investment towards these new "knowledge havens" in a world where expertise and skills are the greatest riches.

As a counterweight, to the need to raise the level of education among the mass public is the need to train talented people who will play a commanding role in steering innovation in a continuously changing technological landscape. We have already looked closely at how university systems in the various corners of the world have gradually addressed the need for excellence in education by identifying national "champions" and setting them apart from other universities, typically giving them greater autonomy, so they are less beholden to local and national rules.

Faced with the accelerating rate of technological and scientific change, it would seem that larger countries and regional districts with homogeneous and centralized governance of university policies (see the United States and China) find that the concentration of private and public resources and freedom in managing their affairs are factors that work to their advantage. Europe, often the epicentre of our analysis in this book, is still adversely affected by fragmented university education policies,

142 Conclusions

so vastly different even within EU boundaries. A policy of discontinuity, which is showing its first very promising green shoots, is to create university education organisms consisting of university networks that would assume power as supranational legal entities and be anchored in EU institutions. There would certainly be benefits in terms of international competition and in defining the model for an interconnected network of universities, which would be different and possibly more dynamic than the model for single academic centres of excellence, in place elsewhere in the world. It is palpably difficult to say how willing European countries would be to cede their sovereignty over an area so critical for the future, but in university education, as elsewhere, the Covid-19 pandemic has spurred European integration in ways inconceivable only a few months ago.

In a medium-to-long-term perspective, today's technological revolution sets challenges to the university education system that are much greater than merely selecting the centres of excellence capable of acting as guides and trailblazers. We can picture a future where the cognitive abilities we currently deem as human are replaced by machines and algorithms, wreaking havoc on the actual concept of skills to be built within higher education. Even creativity, forever seen as a human skill, in some quarters is now being seen as reproducible through the algorithms of artificial intelligence. Chess is a famous case in point: totally new and unexpected moves are seen by judges as a tell-tale sign that the player is being given AI backup, but when teams of only human players, teams of only computers, and mixed humans and AI teams play against each other, the mixed teams win by a country mile. Teaching how to heighten human cognitive power through artificial devices can be a challenge in discontinuity for the university system. It is on par with the challenges faced after the First Industrial Revolution, where not only did people have to be trained to make the machines for automating procedures, but users also had to be shown how the machines could be used in a wide spectrum of applications and so expand their manual skills.

The other great challenge in modern society is certainly the crisis in democratic systems and representation through delegation. While in many countries there is a loss of trust in the abilities of the governing élites, we also note that the political classes seem less able to govern, as we have seen in many countries around the world in relation to the Covid-19 pandemic. Balancing the principle of competence and the principle of majority in educating government leaders has never been easy, but today the problems are more convoluted and bring up further specific questions (Pizzorno, 2013).

It is not unreasonable to conjure up situations where the role played by universities in the evolution of democratic systems can change, so that they expand their functions and even become places for elaborating thought at the service of political and strategic choices. There is obviously the disturbing risk of cliquey oligarchic swerving, as conceived by writers and thinkers who saw a dystopic future ruled exclusively by groups of technocrats. However, the trend to put technical and scientific organisms in charge of directing and supporting wider strategic

Conclusions **143**

choices, a route taken by many countries during the Covid-19 pandemic, opens the imagination to many potential directions of evolution in universities. Technical and scientific institutions, in particular, could take on a more formal role in managing knowledge at the service of political choices, alongside more robust and widespread forms of participation and informed debate, potentially drawing on citizen science, as discussed in Chapter 4 (Della Porta, 2013).

The narrative described, especially the last one, sets the basis for a Third Academic Revolution. As we mentioned in the first chapter of this treatise, after the Second Industrial Revolution, universities went through a First Academic Revolution, expanding their scope from education to research. After the Third Industrial Revolution, universities faced a Second Academic Revolution, this time expanding their mission to innovation and technological transfer. In the upcoming years, recent developments in what we refer to as the Fourth Industrial Revolution, in practice an extension of the third, and probable technological developments in other domains, will encourage scientific and technological universities, especially, to become society's bastion in developing research, technology, skills and, above all, helping to frame long-term public and private policies, therefore going through the Third Academic Revolution.

Many of these evolutionary discontinuity futures, and others that can be imagined, will never come to pass, or may be circumscribed to smaller spheres of action. What we do know is that the pace of technological change, as well as emergency situations and urgencies, prepares the ground for these futures to be possible, and forces those taking decisions about strategic development lines in universities to assess the various risks and opportunities.

5.4 Governing the dynamics of change

Having reached the end of the analysis investigated in this book, we can see that the waters of change in the university world typically flow very slowly and run well beyond the mandate of university officials empowered to make decisions concerning strategic directions. This traditional inertia to change has contributed to fuelling the picture of universities as fundamentally conservative institutions.

We are living in a period in which, for the many reasons analysed, change and innovation within universities seem to be advancing at a decidedly speedy pace. This state of play has delivered into the hands of upper management, in single universities or in entire university systems, the opportunity of truly governing the direction of evolution, as well as taking on the grave responsibility of the associated consequences.

In this text, we do not and cannot make suggestions about any specific direction of travel because every choice is interwoven with its context, but we do wish to embed the urgency of innovation at the core of any analysis of possible strategies. We have described a framework of analysis and proposed a set of decisional levers. Our wish is for them to be a "manual" for decision-makers tomorrow and in the near future.

Chapter references

Della Porta, D. (2013). *Can democracy be saved? Participation, deliberation and social movements.* Cambridge: Polity Press.

Giaccardi, C., & Magatti, M. (2020). *Nella fine è l'inizio. In che mondo vivremo.* Bologna: Il Mulino.

Pizzorno, A. (2013). Competenza e maggioranza nel processo di decisione. In C. Bianchetti & A. Balducci (Eds.), *Competenza e rappresentanza.* Roma: Donzelli.

INDEX

Note: Page numbers in italics indicate a figure and page numbers in bold indicate a table on the corresponding page.

14 crossroads 7, *7*; *see also* crossroads
2020 health crisis 138; *see also* Covid-19

Aachen University *see* RWTH Aachen
academic accelerators 64
academic adhocracy 131
academic and administrative perspectives 132
academic bodies 27; steered toward needs of scientific production 47
academic careers, management type 133
academic community 70, 71, 96
academic disciplines 36
academic and financial autonomy: Politecnico di Milano 86; TU Berlin 84; TU Delft 87; UCL 85
academic governance systems 5
academic incubators *see* incubators
academic networks of excellence 106, 142
academic oligarchies 78
academic organizations, models of governance in 5
academic paths 116, 18
academic positions 74
academic qualifications 113
academic research 45
academic research profile 96
Academic Revolution 44, 56, 143; *see also* Second Academic Revolution; Third Academic Revolution; Fourth Academic Revolution

academic senate 80, 83, 133
academic settings, glass ceiling index **75**
academic strategies in research and education 6; *see also* universities of science and technology, strategic choices for
access to information *see* synchronous or asynchronous involvement
accreditation 27, 79, 86, 87, 119
active learning 104, 113, 115, 120
actors *see* research actors
adhocracy *see* academic adhocracy
administration *see* university administration
Africa 21, 69
Age of Enlightenment *see* Enlightenment
agile working 113
AI *see* artificial intelligence (AI)
Alliance4Tech 106
Amazon.com 91
Anthropocene Epoch 12
APENET 70n26
applying and transferring knowledge: linearity or circularity 100–102
artificial intelligence (AI) 14, 17, 25, 91; creativity reproduced via 142; production of new knowledge via 93; university expansion of research into 129, 130
artificial sciences 58
Asia **4–5**; world's economy concentrated in 11, 15, 21, 47; Europe in competition

146 Index

with 24; research policy in 59; research trials held in 26; *see also* China
asymmetric model of university governance 80, 82, 86
Australia 79; scientific productivity *50*
Australian National University **4**
autonomy: meritocratic 117; *see also* university autonomy
autonomy or control *see* constraints of context and type of organization: autonomy or control
axes *see* three axes model of contemporary universities

Baldridge, J. 78
bibliometric indicators 28, 48, 99, 120
big tech 141
Bleikie, I. 78
Brexit 25, 140

"Cantiere per le Periferie, Il" (building site for the city's out- skirts) 73
capacity for analysis and critical thinking 137
Carnegie Mellon **4**
CentraleSupélec **83**
centrality of the person 137
Chalmers 53, *54,* **83**
chess 142
China 140; Beijing 69; competitiveness of 15; economic domination of 11; growing importance of 140; public university policies of 123, 141; scientific and technological advances by 15, 23, 65; standards of quality in 119; strong national identity of 137; United States and 15, 64, 137; *see also* Shanghai Jiao Tong; Tsinghua
Chinese University of Hong Kong **5**
Clark, B. R. 78
coalface of innovation 108
Coalition of Urban Serving Universities (USU) 71
collaborative global research, ecosystem of 96
"communities of innovation" 67
competence, principle of 142
competencies: assessing 134; building up 136; HR 122; student 36
competition or collaboration *see* working in research (competition or collaboration)
constraints of context and type of organization: autonomy or control 122–125
convergence 97; of organic and inorganic sciences 94; of scientific and technological domains 14, 16, 58–60

core competencies demanded by the job market 2015–2020, changes to *20*
Covid-19 pandemic 2, 75, distance learning during 26, 115; European integration spurred by 142; technological and digital reconsiderations spurred by 112–113, 115, 143; universities' strategic decisions accelerated by 135, 140
crisis 113, 140
crossroads 7–8, 90–134; *see also* picture crossroad
cybernetical studies 59
cyber-physical teaching environment 42

decision-making procedures and resource allocation: direct or indirect 128–131
de-globalization 140
de-industrialization 79
Delft University of Technology **4**; *see also* TU Delft
democratic systems, crisis in 142–143
democratization of university education 28
de-qualification 133
"Didattica sul Campo" (on-field teaching) 73–75
different learning pathways: uniformity or customization 116–118
digital era 60
digital industry: "unicorns" 2, 16
digital networks 58
digital or physical relationships between professors and students 112–116
digital platforms 138
Digital Revolution 61
digital teaching technology 14, 26, 37, 42, 140
digital tools 36, 104, 113, 115, 116, 135, 136, 139
disciplines (fields of), emergence of 59
distributed manufacturing 14
diversity and complementarity 137
diversity, equality, inclusion 69, 73
doctorate studies *see* education and doctorate studies
dual governance structure 80

École Polytechnique Fédérale de Lausanne (EPFL) **5**, 55, **83**, 94n38
economic. . . *see* social and economic development; social and economic divide; social and economic systems
economic and production systems 46, 60
economic change, drivers of *18*
economic crisis 16, 28
economic cycles 47
economic downturn, European Union 137

economic dynamics, global *12*
economic growth 11, 13, 14; North America 21; technology and 45
economics and finances of universities 124
economics (discipline of) 1, 2
Economics, Nobel Prize in 91
economic systems: local versus national 15
economic theory 45; neoclassical 13, 16
economy: financialization of 1; global 15; innovation's role in stimulating 69, 138; knowledge 1, 6, 17, 45, 61, 91; sharing 14; technical education's impact on 37; universities' impact on 2, 27, 79, 117, 129; world 11, 13
ecosystem: of disciplinary skills 97; of collaborative global research 96, 100; economic, social, and knowledge 24; industrial and production 57; innovation 60, 61–64; innovation and research 16; new knowledge 2, 62; social 98; SRU 46; start-up 68; university 58, 93, 98, 99, 138
ecosystems transformation: globalization and 12
educational systems 120–125; technical universities 37–38
education and doctorate studies 55–56
education models 36; evolution of 38–44; in technical universities 37–38; *see also* picture crossroads
education, purpose of 118–120; *see also* universities
EIT *see* European Institute of Innovation & Technology (EIT)
e-learning 112
electricity 11
Enlightenment 9, 10, 11, 59
entrepreneurial innovation 6, 34, 89, 137
entrepreneurial university 57, 61–69; *see also* entrepreneurship
entrepreneurship 34, 42, 46, 47; university 56–58
EPFL *see* École Polytechnique Fédérale de Lausanne (EPFL)
ERC *see* European Research Council 70
ERC Public Engagement with Research Awareness 70
ETH *see* Swiss Federal Institute of Technology (ETH) **5, 83**
Etzkowitz, Henry 63
European Commission's Horizon 2020 programme 73
European history and culture, defining features of 137
European Institute of Innovation & Technology (EIT) 67–68

Europe: scientific productivity *50*; technical innovation in 65; technical universities **4–5**
Europe of knowledge, development of 90
European Research Council 70, 108
European University Initiative 138
excellence: academic centres of 142; "clubs of" 107; factors of 28, 98; high standards of 73; individual 108, 109, 110, 111; investing in 137; need for 141; policies geared toward 106; private schools of 47; researchers of 111; schools of 120; scientific 137, 138
external constraints, system of 122

Far East 27, 48, *50*
FDS Laboratory 71
First Academic Revolution 143
First Industrial Revolution 1, 9, 11, 142
Flexner, Abraham 101
flipped classroom 113, 114
Fordism, post 79
Fourth Industrial Revolution 1, 14–15, 17, 57–58, 61, 143
France 66, 67, 79, 110, 123
Fudan University **4**

Georgia Institute of Technology **4**, 48, 93n37
Germany 23, 26; education system overhaul 45; research doctorates 55; technological innovation led by 65–66; university control in 123; *see also* TU Berlin; TU Munich
Germany-Switzerland axis 24
Giaccardi, C. 140
glass ceiling index (GCI) 74, *75*
global economic dynamics *12*, 29, 47
global innovation index 66, *66*; 2019 score *67*
Google 91, 141
governance models *see* university governance models
governance macro models, geographic distribution of *81*
Grandes Écoles 123
Great Depression 18

Harvard University **4**, *54*
Harvard-MIT Program in Health Sciences and Technology (HST) 93n37
Hoc-Lab 71
Hong Kong University of Science & Technology **5**
human resource organization and management: specialization or integration 131–133

148 Index

Humboldtian model of higher education 6, 79
Humboldt University of Berlin 79
hyperconnectivity 60
hyper-cycle *see* MOOC

IDEA League 106
identity of contemporary universities 5, 7, 94, 96; research system based on 9; student presence defining 114; topics linked to 138; *see also* three axes model of contemporary universities
identity or prominence *see* knowledge development trajectories
Imperial College London **4**, **83**
incubators 42, 43, 64, 68
India 11, 55
inequality 6; economic 64; gender 74; in the right to study 27; social 15, 75, 91; STEM 74
information technologies (IT) 25
InnoEnergy 68
innovation 1; challenges of 38; collaborative global research and 96; consolidated research networks and 109; debate on 26; entrepreneurial 6, 34, 89, 127; Europe as center of 64; Fourth Industrial Revolution 61; gap 45; importance of investing in 123; incremental 98–99; invention and discovery cycle of *102*; models of research and 21–25; promoting 35, 103; regional 33; research and 101–103, 123, 124; Second Academic Revolution triggered by 46; scientific 15, 44; SRUs and 47; systemic 62, 63; system-wide overview of 94; technological 10, 12–13, 16–17, 21, 65; universities' role in fostering or generating 68, 73, 79, 126; *see also* global innovation index
innovation capacity 64
innovation districts 69
innovation ecosystems 60, 63
innovation market 100
innovation paradigms: university entrepreneurship and 56–69
innovation processes 37, 62; drivers of 61; transformation of 59
innovation sphere 133
innovation systems 4, 16, 64, 68, 79, 94
innovation in teaching 113
integration and forms of participation, models *62*
interacting actively or passively in learning and work practices 113

international geopolitical dynamics 139
Internet of People 14
Internet of Things 14
Italy 10; dual traditional university governance model 82; economic and industrial systems of 28; global innovation index, position on 67; Milan 24; national funding 108; private universities 123; public engagement by 70; recruitment process 110; research and development 23; STEM, inequalities in 74, 75; technical university model 37, 79; university excellence 28; university systems and politics 27; university students *11*

junior faculty 82, **83**

KAIST *see* Korea Advanced Institute of Science and Technology (KAIST)
Keynes, J. M. 17
know-how 43, 68, 97
knowledge 7; access and transmission of 61; applying and transferring 100–103; classification and transmission of 11; concepts and models of 9; creating and spreading 121; demand for 102; democratization and diffusion of 26, 28, 69, 70, 73; digital 60; dynamics of creating 26; economic value of 55; entrepreneurial production of 61–63; forms, objectives, and how it develops 90–103; fragmentation of 96; globalized 13; "grey area" of 26; new geographies of 3, 15, 25; polarization of 64; producing and circulating 55, 58; progress of 95; project-based 42; silos of 127; SRUs and 46; students' role in spreading 105; systematic checking of 44; technical 19; theoretical 41; three axes of university development 89–90; universities as producers of 34; verification of 62
knowledge and its boundaries: disciplinarity or hybridization 95–97
knowledge and learning 20, 36; *see also* learning
knowledge as factor in production 79
knowledge as linear process 101
knowledge-based economy and society 91
knowledge development trajectories 98–100
knowledge domains 59, 60, 61
knowledge economy 1, 6, 17, 45, 61, 91
knowledge ecosystems 2, 24

Index **149**

knowledge havens 141
knowledge-intensive activities 91
knowledge transfer 92; processes of 59
knowledge value chain 91
Kogan, M. 78
Korea Advanced Institute of Science and
  Technology (KAIST) **4**
KTH *see* Royal Institute of Technology
  (KTH)
KU Leuven 56
Kyoto University **4**

land-grant universities 79
learning: academic 70; active 104,
  113, 115, 120; complementary 44;
  continuous 19, 128; distance 26, 113;
  inductive forms of 41; knowledge and
  20; life-long 97, 127; multi-disciplinary
  43; online 107, 112, 113, 114; passive
  40, 104, 113, 115, 116; physical spaces
  of 114; teaching and 79; *see* access to
  information; digital teaching technology;
  MOOCs
learning by doing 19
learning by projects 39, 42–43
learning models 41, 63
learning pathways 40; uniformity or
  customization 116–118
learning process 36, 41
learning processes: complex 59
learning society 91; *see also* active learning
Leydesdor, Loet 63
life-cycle of a research topic 99

Magatti, M. 140
Massachusetts Institute of Technology
  (MIT) 48, 54, *54*, 56; as high-tech
  business 63
massive open online courses (MOOCs) 26,
  112–113, 115; hyper-cycle of 113
Master's in Business Administration, model
  of 1, 13n3
master's degree programmes focusing on
  engineering, architecture and design
  37, *39*
master's students as a percentage of all
  incoming students (undergraduates +
  master's students) *40*
master's students, gender balance 73
mental openness and mutual respect 137
MIT *see* Massachusetts Institute of
  Technology (MIT)
Monash University **4**
MOOCs *see* massive open online courses
  (MOOCs)

Narayanamurt, V. 101
National Co-ordinating Centre for Public
  Engagement (NCCPE)
National Science Foundation (NSF) (US)
  101
National Taiwan University **5**
Nanyang Technological University,
  Singapore **5**
National University of Singapore **5**
NCCPE *see* National Co-ordinating
  Centre for Public Engagement
  (NCCPE)
net-based technologies, advent of 17
Netherlands, the 26, 67, 82; *see also* TU Delft
networks: client 14; collaborative 17;
  decentralized 33; digital 58; empowering
  90; FabLab 42; global 24; multi-
  structured 20; neural 59; research
  108–111; strategic 138; university 104,
  107, 113, 135, 136, 138, 142
networks of excellence 106
network of interaction and collaboration
  116, 128
networks of knowledge: global 26, 46
networks of strategic partnerships 118
new public management model 27, 47, 79,
  119, 132
North America **4–5**; scientific productivity
  50

Oceania **4–5**
Odumosu, T. 101
OECD analysis of student socio-economic
  status 120
OECD averages of several countries in R
  &D *22*, *23*, 22–24, 55
online learning 112, 113, 114; aggregators
  107
online university 140
openness or closure (mental) 130, 137
organizational architecture 125–128;
  purpose of education: rights or merits
  118–120
outreach programmes 34, 69–73
overview by universities 71

passive learning 40, 104, 113, 115, 116;
  see also learning
Pasteur's quadrant *103*
patents 22, 23; percentages submitted,
  global with focus on Europe *65*, 66
path dependency 119
Peking University **4**
personalization and differentiation *see* study
  paths

150 Index

petroleum 11

physical interaction and interaction mediated through digital tools 113

picture crossroad: applying and transferring knowledge (linearity or circularity) 100–102; constraints of context and type of organization (autonomy or control) 122–125; decision-making procedures and resource allocation (direct or indirect) 128–131; different learning pathways (uniformity or customization) 116–118; educational systems 120–125; human resource organization and management (specialization or integration) 131–133; knowledge and its boundaries (disciplinarity or hybridization) 95–97; knowledge development trajectories (identity or prominence) 97–100; organizational architecture 125–128; purpose of education (rights or merits) 118–120; relationship between professors and students (digital or physical) 111–116; research actors (stars or teams) 109–111; universities and professional growth 134; working in research (competition or collaboration) 107–109

Polisocial 72

Politecnico di Milano (PoliMI) 2040 i, vi, vii 2–3, 56, **83**; governance 85–86; initiatives 71–73; prominence *54*

Princeton **4**; Institute for Advanced Study 101

private equity funds 68

private schools of excellence 47

private sector 57, 124

private universities 108, 123

prominence maps 53, *54*

prominence of topics *53*

public and private. . ..: actors 25, 100; collaborations 67; dichotomy 122; divide 9; finances 21; funding 45; policies 6, 34, 143; resources 5, 141; sector 137; shareholding 122; stakeholders 16; universities 123

public debate 35; universities engaged in 69, 70, 114

public engagement by universities 69–73, 127–128

public management model *see* new public management model

public research centres 22

public service organizations 27

public spending and investment 15, 21, 26–28, 46

public underwriting 125

public universities: engagement by 69–73, 127–128; policies 33; quality assurance models utilized by 117; tenure at 124

relationships: axis of 89–90, 103–104, 140, 141; hierarchical 122; internal and external 7; long term working 95, 109; social 44; strategic 60; systems of 5, 17, 24, 68

relationship ecosystem 62

relationship between. . ..: academia and local communities 63; economic and social actors 64; professors and students 111–116; theory and practice 41–42; universities and stakeholders 35; university and state 78

research actors: stars or teams 109–111

research doctors in several countries, comparisons *55, 56, 57*

research networks *see* networks

research topics: balancing focus and prominence 51–54

resource allocation 128–131

resource availability 121, 139

resource organization *see* human resource organization and management

Royal Institute of Technology (KTH) **4**

RWTH Aachen University **4**, *54*, **56, 83**

science, technology, engineering and mathematics (STEM subjects) 55; inequalities in 74–75

scientific productivity 47–51; in Europe, North America, Far East and Australia *49–50*; percentage variation in productivity *51, 52*

scientific research 44–47

Second Academic Revolution 46, 57, 143

Second Industrial Revolution 1, 10–12, 45, 56, 79, 93, 143

Second World War 11

Seoul National University **4**

Shanghai Jao Tong University **4**, 48, *54*

sharing economy 14

She Figures 2018 73–74, *74*

Singapore 24, 123; Nanyang Technological University, Singapore **5**; National University of Singapore **5**

SJTU *54*

skill renewal 19

skills: basic 114; cognitive 19; core 36; creativity seen as 142; critical 26; design 60; disciplinary 95–97; future 25; high specialist 140; interpersonal 141; job-related 28, 41, 79, 118, 140; knowledge

economy and 17; management 132; manual 43; micro- 141; multi-disciplinary 42; need to update 16, 20; organizational 42; professional 141; social transformation of 18; technical and scientific 106, 120; transversal 36; universities as suppliers of 139, 142, 143; validation of 117; vertical specialization of 132
skillsets 17, 44, 120; management 133
social acceptance 62
social actors 64
social and economic constraints 79
social and economic development 24, 66; accelerators 58
social and economic divides 25, 75
social and economic fabric 92, 99
social and economic landscapes 28, 89, 126
social and economic status 120
social and economic systems 6, 17, 60, 137, 138, 139
social ecosystems 95, 98; transformation of 12; universities and 24, 58, 69, 92
social hybridization 12
social inequality 15
social intelligence 18
social interaction 112, 114, 115
socialization structures 97
social outreach 69, 89
social policies and health 15
social progress 139
social responsibility 35
social sciences 1, 13, 16m 53, 59, 60, 94
social toolkit 116
social value of universities 34; actions related to 35
social well-being 45
spending per student and percentage of funding sources 46
space research (i.e. outer space) 91
spaces: co-working 68; European knowledge 105; integrated 43; learning 42, 114; market 140, 141; social 116; teaching 116; testing 26
Space X 91
SPOCs 26
SRU see Super Research University (SRU)
Stanford 54, 56, 63
start-up incubators 68
status and staff recruitment see university status and staff recruitment
steam engine 11
strategic choices 7, 24, 142; see also universities of science and technology, strategic choices for

strategic decisions 61, 80, 135, 138, 143
strategic guidelines 5, 70, 130
strategic objectives 27, 34
strategic orientation tool 8
strategic partnerships 40, 106
strategic planning 4
strategic priorities 21
strategic settings 5
strategic vision 2, 84, 140
steering at a distance 79, 125
steering researchers and research strategies 24, 29, 59, 99, 110; importance of strategic vision 140
STEM see science, technology, engineering and mathematics (STEM subjects)
Stiglitz, Joseph 91
structure and organizational autonomy see university structure and organizational autonomy
students see relationships between. . .: professors and students
students in tertiary education worldwide, time series from 1970 to 2018 10
students in university in Italy, time series from 1869 to 2014 11
study paths: personalization and differentiation in 39–41
Super Research University (SRU) 45–47
Sweden 67, 119
Swiss Federal Institute of Technology (ETH) 5, 83
Switzerland 47, 61, 67, 82, 123
synchronous or asynchronous involvement 104, 113, 115
systemic innovation 62, 63
systemic view 19
systems: academic 5, 139; academic governance 5; axes of 89–90; bureaucratic 125; cognitive technologies and biological 59; economic 12, 15, 21, 23, 25, 63; educational 13, 34, 45, 104, 119; external constraints 122; financial 14; governance 78–80, 82–87; innovation 4, 16, 64, 68, 79, 94; local 4; Italian industrial 28; management-control 130; many-actor 66; monochromatic 124; national university 120; research 99, 108; social 60; specialization of 9; supervisory 111; supranational 4; uniform 138; university 3, 13, 24, 25–26, 36, 37, 44, 119–125, 140; university organizational model 7–8, 135; value 138

152 Index

teaching: bolstering of 139; experimental 72, 73; pre- and post-degree 91; traditional 112; *see also* active learning; learning; passive learning
teaching and research 25–26, 28, 34, 45; careers oriented toward 118; collaborative models based on complementarity in 93, 94; competition and cooperation in 107; digital tools for 135; disciplinary integration in 96–97; Humboldt's combination of 79; international 132; inter-subject integration in 92; networked 104, 109; self-reliance in 136; strategies 127, 128; technical and scientific 121; technical universities, future of 103; as traditional cornerstones of academic work 71
teaching and the right to study 124
teaching faculty 109; recruitment of 106
teaching in presence 114
teaching methodologies 36
teaching methods, interactive 39
teaching models 38, 40–41; inductive 42; participatory 41
teaching resources, allocation of 131, 138
teaching staff 55, 70; demotivation among 125; *see also* university status and staff recruitment
teaching techniques, rethinking of 113
teaching toolkit 116
teaching units 44
teaching universities 9
technical universities **4–5**; education in 37–38; *see also* universities of science and technology
technological advancement 13
technological decoupling, Sino-American 64
technological change, drivers of 19, *19*
technological innovation 10, 12–13, 16–17; critical importance of 65; discontinuities in sphere of 64; radical change at core of 58; theory of endogenous growth and 13; work and 21
technological transfer 4, 21, 34, 45, 46; demand for 102; Etzkowitz and 63; universities and 129
technology: advanced 45; changes in the nature of 17, 19; digital 16; as driver of innovation 60; information 13; nanotechnology 16; network 1, 14, 36; publications in the field of 48, *52*; rapid evolution of 42
technology foresight studies and centers 100
Technology Readiness Levels (TRLs) 101

tenure, concept of 124
tenured faculty **83**
Third Academic Revolution 143
Third Industrial Revolution 1, 12–13, 15–16, 57, 93, 143
three axes model of contemporary universities 5–7, 89–90, *90*; *see also* knowledge; relationships; system
Tokyo Institute of Technology **4**
top 50 university cities *25*
traditional university self-governance model 79–80, 82
trailblazing 108, 139, 142
Triple Helix model 63
Tsinghua University 48, *54*
TU Berlin 56, 82, **83**; governance 83–84
TU Delft *54*, 82, **83**; governance 86–87
tuition fees: Politecnico di Milano 86; TU Berlin 84; TU Delft 87; UCL 85
TU Munich 56

UBI Global 68
undergraduate degree programmes focusing on engineering, architecture and design *38*; *see also* STEM
unitary governance structure 80
United Kingdom 26, 28, 78; new public management model 79; public engagement by 71; recruitment process 110; research doctorates produced by 55; *see also* University College London
United States: China and 64, 65; crises in financial markets 15; "excel to compete" 105; job profiles in 17; land-grant universities 79; National Science Foundation 101; public urban research universities 71; research trials 26; research doctorates produced by 55; research quality in 28; standards of quality 119; technocratic approach of 59; technological universities 45; *see also* Harvard; MIT; Princeton; Stanford
universities and professional growth 134
universities: as "clubs for excellence" 107; in competition or collaboration 107–109; for the elite 104, 121; European *83*; human resource organization and management 131–133; Italian *82*; learning pathways offered by 116–118; for the masses 104, 121; open 104; organizational architecture 125–128; organizational types 122–125; pathways of professional growth 134; professors and students 112–116; recruitment of researchers 111; resource allocation

128–131; self-standing or sharing 104–107; self-sufficient or contained 103; *see also* educational systems; research networks; teaching and research; teaching universities; technical universities
universities of science and technology, strategic choices for 91; *see also* picture crossroad
university administration 27, 78, 124, 131–132; apparatus 45
university autonomy: six broad areas 123–125
University College London (UCL) **4, 83,** 84–85
university fees 27
university governance, comparisons among European countries *81*
university governance models: comparisons among four European institutions 80–87; three main types 78
University of Berlin 79
University of California, Berkeley **4**
University of California Los Angeles **4**
University of Hong Kong **5**
University of Illinois at Urbana-Champaign **4**

University of Melbourne **4**
University of Michigan – Ann Arbor **5**
University of New South Wales **4**
University of Oxford **4**
University of Sidney **4**
University of Texas at Austin **5**
University of Tokyo **4**
University of Toronto **5**
university status and staff recruitment: Politecnico di Milano 86; TU Berlin 84; TU Delft 87; UCL 85
university structure and organizational autonomy: Politecnico di Milano 85; TU Berlin 83; TU Delft 86; UCL 84
university town 140
USU *see* Coalition of Urban Serving Universities (USU)

vital catastrophe 140

Wharton School of Business 13n3
working in research: competition or collaboration 107–109
World War II 10

Zhejiang University **4**

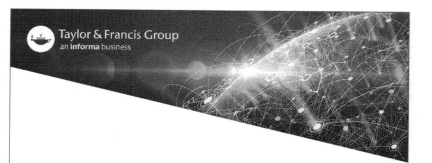

Printed in the United States
by Baker & Taylor Publisher Services